"Building on the principle in ecumenical dialogue of an exchange of gifts, Durheim develops a methodology of theological enrichment by which an awareness of theological resonances may lead toward mutually beneficial insights. His study of the sacramental theology and ethics of Luther and Chauvet gives flesh to this methodology, thus not only exposing and advancing current thinking about these two theologians but also helping to build bridges between Lutherans and Roman Catholics today. Readers interested in ecumenical engagement, sacramental theology, Christian ethics, and the interrelations of these three will appreciate Durheim's fresh approach."

— Karen Westerfield Tucker
Boston University

"This very timely and creative work brings together key items on the contemporary theological scene—sacraments, ethics, ecumenism, and the approaching anniversary of the Protestant Reformation. It sparks flashes of new insight into theology and the practical Christian life. Durheim repositions the heirs of the great reformer Martin Luther and of Catholicism's Thomas Aquinas, replacing the original Reformation battle over faith and works, grace and free will, individual believer and sacramental system with a rich exchange. Here, differences yield a mutual expansion of horizons, not a standoff of mutual condemnation. Durheim's fresh and unusual sacramental theology speaks to the global justice questions so vital to today's faithful and their churches. For both Luther and Louis-Marie Chauvet the sacraments mediate God's gift of transformed Christian action. With Chauvet, Durheim insists that faith is meaningless without commitment to social justice; with Luther, he reminds us that progress is entirely reliant on God's grace. *Christ's Gift, Our Response* will reward all who value the integration of theology, liturgy, and life."

— Lisa Sowle Cahill
Boston College

"Durheim's *Christ's Gift, Our Response* offers readers on both sides of the Tiber an opportunity for theological enrichment. The theology of Luther and his contemporary interpreters is set alongside that of the contemporary French Catholic Chauvet, a thinker influenced by postmodern philosophy and such heirs of Lutheran thought as Heidegger and Nietzsche. Durheim does not argue for a unified thesis concerning the Eucharist and ethics but rather demonstrates where Chauvet and Luther, Catholics and Protestants, and postmoderns and late medievalists can begin to see each other as sources of insight. Such is necessary for those who wish both to increase their own faith and to work toward a more unified Christian community."

— Dr. Jennifer Hockenbery Dragseth
Professor of Philosophy
Mount Mary University

"In this book, Benjamin Durheim builds bridges, creatively and with sensitivity, for theological resonance between thinkers one might rarely see in dialogue—Martin Luther and Louis-Marie Chauvet. His analysis of their theology, their questions and tensions, opens up areas of surprising consensus and continued challenges. Durheim is able, to use his own phrase, 'to establish a common basis for theological exchange in the connection between sacraments and ethics.'"

— Dirk G. Lange
Associate Professor of Worship
Luther Seminary

Christ's Gift, Our Response

Martin Luther and Louis-Marie Chauvet on the
Connection between Sacraments and Ethics

Benjamin Durheim

A Michael Glazier Book

LITURGICAL PRESS

Collegeville, Minnesota

www.litpress.org

A Michael Glazier Book published by Liturgical Press

Excerpts from documents of the Second Vatican Council are from *Vatican Council II: The Conciliar and Postconciliar Documents*, edited by Austin Flannery, OP, © 1996. Used with permission of Liturgical Press, Collegeville, Minnesota.

Excerpts from "The Babylonian Captivity of the Church" and "Against the Fanatics" from *Word and Sacrament II*, vol. 36 of *Luther's Works*, ed. Abdel Ross Wentz and Helmut T. Lehmann (Fortress Press, 1959). Used by permission of Augsburg Fortress Publishers.

1	2	3	4	5	6	7	8	9

Library of Congress Cataloging-in-Publication Data

Durheim, Benjamin M.
    Christ's gift, our response : Martin Luther and Louis-Marie Chauvet on the connection between sacraments and ethics / Benjamin M. Durheim.
      pages cm
    "A Michael Glazier book."
    Includes bibliographical references and index.
    ISBN 978-0-8146-8323-1 — ISBN 978-0-8146-8348-4 (ebook)
      1. Sacraments—Catholic Church. 2. Sacraments—Lutheran Church.
3. Christian ethics. 4. Chauvet, Louis-Marie, 1941– 5. Luther, Martin, 1483–1546. 6. Catholic Church—Relations—Lutheran Church.
7. Lutheran Church—Relations—Catholic Church. I. Title.

BX2200.D845   2015
234'.16—dc23
                                2014049742

Contents

Chapter 2

Sacraments and Ethics in Martin Luther   41

Chapter 3

Sacraments and Ethics in Louis-Marie Chauvet   77

Chapter 4

Conversation between Luther and Chauvet   111

Acknowledgments

There are many people whose support and tireless work have aided me in completing this book, without which it would not have been possible. I would like especially to thank John Baldovin, SJ, who provided invaluable comments, input, and insight as I worked to finish this project. Lisa Cahill and Shawn Copeland, as well as Richard Gaillardetz and Dirk Lange, provided both conversation and written comments without which the book could not have been what it is. I am also tremendously thankful for the theological formation I have been fortunate enough to receive both at Boston College and previously at Saint John's School of Theology and Seminary. The faculty, staff, and student communities have been instrumental in making me the theologian I am trying to be. There are far too many names to be able to mention them all, but in particular I would like to thank David Turnbloom, Kevin Ahern, and Nicole Reibe for their collegial assistance and camaraderie in our shared journey. Additionally, I would like to thank Hans Christoffersen, Lauren L. Murphy, and Liturgical Press for their support and help in making this book a reality. I would also like to thank my family—particularly my parents and sister—for their steadfast faith in me.

Finally and most significantly, my wife Tara has given me more help than I can recount. She has shared in my triumphs and my frustrations as this book project has unfolded, and has never wavered in her confidence in me. She has been a patient sounding board, an enthusiastic cheerleader, and a fantastic editor. For these and all the other innumerable ways she has helped me, I thank her.

Introduction

The goal of this book is, in the first place, ecumenical. As the five hundredth anniversary of the beginning of the Protestant Reformation approaches, questions of what it means to worship and live as a Christian community ecclesially divided from other Christian communities takes on renewed poignancy. The relationship of Christian worship (particularly sacraments) to Christian ethical life cannot be answered as if the term "Christian" were a generic term divorced from particular theological, sacramental, and ethical traditions. As such, this book focuses on a pair of theologians representing theological approaches of two Christian communions: Lutheranism and Roman Catholicism. Drawing on other traditions could certainly also be helpful, but these two traditions represent both the inception of the Protestant Reformation and some of the most sustained work in subsequent ecumenical engagement and dialogue. In this light, the central aim of this book is to build a new bridge across the Tiber (or at least to refurbish a neglected one) for theology in sacraments and ethics. Ideally, this will be a bridge over which insights can be transported without succumbing to the all-too-familiar pitfalls of Lutheran–Roman Catholic dialogue in these fields of theology.[1] Toward this end, the book works to establish a common basis for theological exchange in the connection between sacraments and ethics and tests the bridge by actually transporting some insights across—insights that can lend enrichment to each distinct side.

---

[1] E.g., forensic justification, causality, merit, and others. Such terms are discussed in this project, but the conversation is not built on them.

Why This Project?

One might rightly ask a significant question at the beginning of this project: why is a bridge across the Tiber a good idea at all? Without attempting to singlehandedly justify the Ecumenical Movement, we nevertheless ought to name some reasons this particular project is important. First, the field of sacramental theology has consistently been a source of theological tension between Lutherans and Roman Catholics, even when consensus is reached in other areas of theology. For example, the 1541 *Regensburger Buch* reached a remarkable consensus on the doctrine of justification but was ultimately rejected by both Luther and Rome because it failed to reach a similar consensus on the theology of the Eucharist.[2] What could have been a significant step in church unity instead stumbled over sacramental theology and yielded very little progress.

In a striking parallel, while the Lutheran World Federation and the Roman Catholic Church were able in 1999 to publish together the *Joint Declaration on the Doctrine of Justification*, the 1978 document of the Lutheran–Roman Catholic Dialogue on the Eucharist did not provide sufficient common ground for any visible unity in celebration, and by 2014 the Dialogue has only moved to the issue of baptism.[3] In both the Colloquy of Regensburg and the current Lutheran–Roman Catholic Dialogue it is not soteriology that has prevented moving toward an expression of visible church unity but rather sacramental theology. If visible church division is a central ecumenical problem, then it is worship and sacraments—the embodied, visible actions of the church—that have played and continue to play a definitive role in how that problem can be addressed.

Second, talking across the Tiber about sacraments is a central part of the Lutheran–Roman Catholic Dialogue leading up to 2017. The Lutheran–Roman Catholic Commission on Unity has published a theological commemoration titled *From Conflict to Communion: Lutheran-Catholic*

---

[2] The Lutheran World Federation and the Pontifical Council for Promoting Christian Unity, *From Conflict to Communion: Lutheran-Catholic Common Commemoration of the Reformation in 2017* (Leipzig, Germany: Evangelische Verlagsanstalt, 2013), 34. For a more in-depth study of the Colloquy of Regensberg, see Suzanne Hequet, *The 1541 Colloquy at Regensburg: In Pursuit of Church Unity* (Saarbrücken, Germany: VDM Verlag, 2009).

[3] See the summaries at http://www.lutheranworld.org/content/lutheran-roman -catholic-dialogue.

Common Commemoration of the Reformation in 2017, which names baptism as the core basis for common commemoration.[4] Common commemoration is, however, neither consensus nor communion. If communion is part of the ecumenical project, then continued and creative work in sacramental theology will be essential. In the context of this book, I attempt what I hope is some level of that creativity in building a bridge for theological resonance rather than consensus. Beyond the raw importance of sacramental theology, the reason this project unfolds as it does is because nearly half a millennium of searching for consensus in sacramental theology has simply not yielded it. Perhaps another approach—searching for resonance rather than confluence—will provide some small ways of moving forward where there previously had been none.

The intention is not to pretend that the search for theological resonance is a new approach to ecumenism. Rather, if the primary goal of an ecumenical conversation can be to strive to determine how each theology might *strengthen* the other rather than just how they might possibly coexist, the dynamic of the conversation changes from working across from one's conversation partner to working alongside one another. This does not mean collapsing theological positions together as if there were no differences. Instead, it means critically accessing the thought of one's partner as a source, not with the goal of creating communion, but with the goal of enriching one's own theological standpoint. An example of one dialogue that did this almost by accident is the lens for this project's engagement with Luther: the Finnish School of Luther Interpretation. Engagement with Orthodox Christians led to new insights in Luther scholarship, precipitating a point of contact between the two communions that had not previously existed. If ecumenical engagement cannot synthesize unity or communion by working toward them as goals, then perhaps unity and communion may grow if they are *not* the initial and immediate goals of ecumenical conversation. Let theological enrichment be the goal, and let communion be the byproduct—not vice versa.

Another major question one ought to ask at the beginning of this project has to do with its second aspect: why study the connection between sacraments and *ethics*? I chose that connection as the subject for this project because it is the connection between what are arguably the two most visible aspects of the church: its worship and the lives of its

---

[4] *From Conflict to Communion*, 80–87.

members in society. If, as *Unitatis Redintegratio* states, "[ecclesial] division openly contradicts the will of Christ, scandalizes the world, and damages that most holy cause, the preaching of the Gospel,"[5] then theological exchange in the most visible aspects of ecclesial life would be a fitting place to attempt to push back that division, scandal, and damage. This is not to say that the concept of the *invisible* church is unnecessary; it is certainly important, especially for Lutheran traditions. It is instead to say that if division is a scandal within the church and for its relationship to the world, then the fields that embody those areas—sacraments and ethics—ought to be ideal places for conversation.

Why Luther and Chauvet?

If the goal of this book is a Lutheran–Roman Catholic conversation on sacraments and ethics that is to resist simply rehearsing the traditional points and counterpoints of sacramental theology and how humans respond to God's action in grace, then the theologies on which the conversation is based should also resist emphasizing those traditional points and counterpoints. As such, this project takes as its hermeneutical approach a relatively new interpretation of Luther, itself born out of an ecumenical conversation, and a late-modern Roman Catholic theologian, whose work both engages traditional sources and also departs from them in certain ways.

The Finnish School of Luther Interpretation grew out of conversations between Finnish Lutheranism and Orthodox Christianity. A more developed background of the School is laid out in chapter 1, but the reason this book takes the Finnish School as its hermeneutical lens for reading Luther is its consistent emphasis on justification as unification with Christ rather than justification as divine imputation. Divine imputation (sometimes called forensic justification) is not utterly alien or contradictory to the Finnish School, but it is also not simply the same idea in different words. By shifting the emphasis in justification away from the external action of God and toward the action of God as uniting with the human, the Finnish School opens up Lutheran theology for a more robust engagement with theologies that tend to highly value

---

[5] Vatican Council II, *Unitatis Redintegratio: Decree on Ecumenism*, para. 1. All citations of documents from the Second Vatican Council are taken from *Vatican Council II: The Conciliar and Postconciliar Documents*, ed. Austin Flannery, rev. ed. (Collegeville, MN: Liturgical Press, 2014).

human participation in justification. This is not an abandonment of Lutheran soteriology or theological anthropology[6] but rather a reading of Luther that is valid alongside the more traditional reading of justification by divine imputation. The result is the ability to read Luther in parallel with a Roman Catholic conversation partner and focus on a particular set of issues in sacraments and ethics that would be clouded by returning only to the Luther of justification by divine imputation, namely, the issues of the gift, ethics and passivity, and the communality of sacraments and ethics.

The Roman Catholic interlocutor that provides an ideal parallel to the Finnish School is the French priest Louis-Marie Chauvet. Like the Finnish School, Chauvet represents something of a departure from what is usually considered the more classic theologies of his ecclesial tradition. Chauvet's theology lifts up the concepts of the symbol and symbolic exchange as his starting points, in an effort to depart from what he sees as an overemphasis on causality in sacramental theology and theologies of grace. Growing out of this re-emphasis is a theological construction of Christian identity centered on the three building blocks of scripture, sacraments, and ethics, which makes Chauvet's construction perfect for the purposes of this book. Further, the symbol and symbolic exchange for Chauvet include an aspect of receiving the presence of the giver within the exchange itself, which provides a foundational point of contact with the "unification" spoken of by the Finnish School.

Apart from these reasons to build this project on the Finnish School of Luther Interpretation and Louis-Marie Chauvet, there still remains the issue of historical distance between Chauvet and Luther. Luther wrote in the sixteenth century, and Chauvet is still alive in the twenty-first. Words, traditions, and the reigning philosophical and theological problems have all gone through multiple centuries of development and change since Luther, so to plop him into a conversation with a late-

---

[6] Other scholars would argue that the Finnish School is exactly this. See William W. Schumacher, *Who Do I Say That You Are? Anthropology and the Theology of* Theosis *in the Finnish School of Tuomo Mannermaa* (Eugene, OR: Wipf and Stock, 2010). That said, such critiques of the Finnish School often tend to treat Luther as more systematic and consistent than his theology actually permits. It is my opinion that Luther's theology lends itself to a multiplicity of interpretations, which need not be seen as contradictory. Consequently, I treat the Finnish School as a legitimately distinct but not hostile interpretation of Luther to that of justification by divine imputation and build this project on it accordingly.

modern figure without attending in some respect to the distance between them would be unfair to the insights of both. That said, there are three main ways the book resists this unfairness. First, the lens through which Luther's theology enters this conversation is that of a late-modern theological movement, the Finnish School. The book does not pretend to apprehend the "true" sixteenth-century Luther and bring him into a conversation that would be largely outside his vocabulary. Instead, the book adopts the major tenets of a school of Luther interpretation that has its own conversation partners in the twenty-first century. It is true that Chauvet and the Finnish School have thus far had essentially no contact with each other, but their historical contexts are far more similar than Luther's is to Chauvet.

Second, in the places where the book *does* attempt to bring Luther into more or less direct conversation with Chauvet, the terms it employs to do this (e.g., the gift or presence) are studied carefully for their meanings in each theologian. On the basis of these studies, the book then presumes to help Chauvet and Luther to "talk" with one another. Further, where there is some commonality in terms, the book looks behind those terms to the theological agendas each thinker has in using them. For example, in chapter 4 when the book speaks of presence, Luther's concern is of the presence of Christ's promise, while Chauvet's is of the presence of Christ's absence. Yet even in these different concerns, there are points common to both approaches, to which the book then attends.

Third, with regard to the many terms that Luther and Chauvet do *not* hold in common, the book does not juxtapose them as if they do. Terms such as justification and symbolic exchange do not commonly appear in the work of both theologians, and where they might they do not mean exactly the same things. As such, these terms are used to orient each theology independently from the other, with the aim of looking for confluence only in terms where it is possible, and even then only with qualification. The goal of this book is to recognize resonances and appreciate mutual enrichment, not to attempt an amalgamation of the theologies.

Brief Overview of the Project

The first chapter begins with an introduction to the twentieth-century field of liturgy and ethics. While the goal of the book as a whole is particularly the connection between *sacraments* and ethics, the shared territory between sacraments and liturgy is considerable. The Liturgical

Movement in North America (particularly in the United States) takes center stage in its reassertion of the connection between liturgy and social justice. Figures such as Virgil Michel and Dorothy Day emphasized the connection between the liturgical celebrations of the church and its call to justice with particular fervor, even as the Liturgical Movement in Europe tended to underemphasize this connection. The chapter then moves to three contemporary theologians whose work is indebted to and yet goes beyond the work of the Liturgical Movement: Don E. Saliers, J.-M.-R. Tillard, and Bruce Morrill. The chapter concludes by placing Chauvet in his philosophical context and naming his major influences and by outlining the major points of the Finnish School of Luther Interpretation as well as the more traditional interpretations of Luther.

The second chapter examines the relevant areas of Luther's theology for the purposes of this discussion. The hermeneutic of the Finnish School is essentially assumed in this chapter, since it was outlined in chapter 1. Chapter 2 works through Luther's sacramental theology, especially under the terms of God's gifts of promise and presence, and then turns to the connection of sacraments and ethics as unification with Christ. Following the Finnish School, Luther's *Commentary on Galatians* serves as the guiding light for this section, giving content to what Luther means by justification and how that unfolds between sacraments and ethics, especially in light of Luther's view of the human as *simul iustus et peccator* (at the same time sinner and justified). Additionally, the chapter appropriates what it can from the more traditional interpretations of Luther, particularly the importance of death and life language, and a view of sanctification as "getting used to" being justified.

The third chapter studies the connection between sacraments and ethics in Chauvet. As two-thirds of Chauvet's tripartite model of Christian identity, Chauvet's views of sacraments and ethics depend heavily on his more foundational tenets of the symbol and his theological anthropology. As such, the first two sections of the chapter attend to how Chauvet conceives of these two areas, at which point the third section can more adequately study how sacraments and ethics interact in Chauvet's thought. Even as the symbol and theological anthropology provide the background for how Chauvet deals with sacraments and ethics, the concepts of the gift and grace emerge as the primary lenses through which he views the connection between sacraments and ethics. Having brought these terms to the fore, chapter 3 concludes with a setup for the fourth chapter.

The fourth and final chapter fleshes out the central goal of this book: a search for resonance and theological exchange between these two theologies that would be enriching for both of them in how they describe the connection between sacraments and ethics. To do this, the chapter names a common principle that both theologians hold—namely, the gift—and then studies tensions in both Luther and Chauvet that could be eased by appropriating certain aspects of the other's thought. For example, Luther's ethics tends to emphasize passivity to Christ's activity (which could lead to despair of one's own ethical action), and Chauvet's conception of the human person can at times seem to lack substantial content (which can lead to ethical complacency). Each theologian can offer insights to assist with these tensions in the other, and the chapter works to facilitate this assistance.

The conclusion then serves as a brief assessment of what has been accomplished. Quickly delineating the high points of each chapter, the conclusion shows how the goal of seeking out resonances and mutual enrichment between these two thinkers has found expression in the book and gestures toward some ways these resonances provide new or expanded areas for ecumenical conversation and work. Altogether, what this book offers is not unity between the thought of Luther and Chauvet—not even in this particular field of sacraments and ethics. Instead, the book provides a conversation between Luther and Chauvet whereby the traditions they represent might approach one another as sources of insight, critically appropriating the contributions each has to offer while remaining faithful to the theologies each embodies. Unity is not the goal, but my hope is that in some way, a kind of unity in theological purpose might nevertheless emerge as the result.

Chapter 1

Background:
The Field of Liturgy and Ethics

Introduction

As the goal of this book is to draw into conversation Luther and Chauvet on the connection between sacraments and ethics, it is necessary to delineate how exactly such a conversation fits into the field of liturgy and ethics as a whole. Additionally, some conception of how and in what light the book will appropriate the work of these theologians, as well as the background that informs such a decision, will serve to set up the studies of chapters 2 and 3. Toward that end, this first chapter proceeds in four parts: first, the chapter traces the origins of renewed theological interest and work in liturgy and ethics, especially in the twentieth century. Second, the chapter gestures toward three current directions in theological scholarship concerning liturgy and ethics, with the goal of situating the current project within that milieu. Third, the chapter outlines Chauvet's philosophical background, providing a springboard for more explicit attention to his theology in the third chapter; fourth, the chapter situates the current project between two strains of interpretation of Luther: the New Finnish Interpretation of Luther, on the one hand, and what has been called "radical Lutheranism," on the other. Having done this, the project can proceed with its goal, reading Chauvet and Luther in light of each other on sacraments and ethics and allowing points of mutual enrichment to emerge.

Background: Liturgy and Ethics

While the relationship between liturgy and ethics has never been alien to Christian theological reflection, it took on renewed significance as a particular area of theological inquiry during the Liturgical Movement of the twentieth century. Especially in the United States, the conviction that what happens within the liturgy is intrinsically connected to the ways by which Christians engage and shape their societies became a theological tenet for many scholars of the Liturgical Movement. This first section of the chapter traces the social and theological circumstances that gave rise to such a tenet and briefly surveys the impacts of two central figures who embodied it: Virgil Michel and Dorothy Day. Having done this, the section traces the development of the emerging discipline of liturgy and ethics through the Second Vatican Council and finally outlines some contemporary directions in theology that are indebted to and participate in the field.

The Liturgical Movement

In its European origins, the Liturgical Movement was a theological expression of a nineteenth-century Christianity struggling to react to the challenges of modernity while rediscovering (and increasingly embracing) the concept of the church as the Mystical Body of Christ.[1] Particularly in Roman Catholic theology, strong reactions against the intellectual creativity of the Enlightenment and Modernism (embodied in part by the First Vatican Council in 1869–70, and more completely by the requirement of the Anti-Modernist Oath beginning in 1910) had the effect of channeling much of the church's creative theological reflection into liturgical theology. Study of the liturgy, right, wrong, or otherwise, was a field of inquiry in which theological development could and did take place. In France, widespread liturgical changes and reforms appeared in response to what were seen as pastoral needs, and in the aftermath of the French Revolution, renewed ecclesial attention to monasticism accomplished the dual task of reviving monastic liturgy and sparking interest in its study, particularly at the Benedictine abbey of Solesmes.[2] In Germany, Benedictine monks such as Odo Casel and Kunibert Mohlberg guided study of the liturgy toward a greater appreciation of the church as the Mystical Body of Christ, and in Belgium,

---

[1] Keith F. Pecklers, *The Unread Vision: The Liturgical Movement in the United States of America* (Collegeville, MN: Liturgical Press, 1998), 1.
[2] Ibid., 2–4.

emphasis on active participation became a hallmark of the movement thanks to the work of theologians like Lambert Beauduin and events such as the National Congress of Catholic Works.[3] Nevertheless, while these European geneses of the Liturgical Movement certainly provided a basis for what was to come, none of them stressed the connection of liturgy to justice and ethics with the fervor of the Liturgical Movement in the United States.[4]

The Liturgical Movement in the United States, while it embraced fundamental tenets like active participation that it imported from its European counterparts, ultimately grew into its context by stressing the integral link between liturgy and social justice. An increasingly urbanized and industrialized United States had by the 1920s become a juggernaut of *laissez-faire* capitalism that idolized the individual.[5] Additionally, wealth distribution had become increasingly uneven, a trend that was thrown into tragic relief during the years of the Great Depression following the 1929 stock market crash. While unemployment soared and persevered throughout the 1930s,[6] Christians—particularly Roman Catholics, whose sense of religious identity had enjoyed something of a revival in the 1920s—increasingly sought a sense of community and belonging in their churches, as opposed to within the secular society that had become such a bleak, isolating place.[7] The concept of the Mystical Body of Christ provided fertile ground for theological reflection on this juxtaposition between Christian membership in church and the

---

[3] Ibid., 8–12.

[4] This is not to say that the European Liturgical Movement was devoid of attention to social justice. Certainly, major figures (such as Lambert Beauduin) were greatly influenced by the ethical challenges occasioned by the Industrial Revolution, the pushback of papal encyclicals such as *Rerum Novarum* in 1891, and eventually the work of figures like Virgil Michel and Dorothy Day.

[5] Pecklers, *The Unread Vision*, 82–84. See also Glenn Porter, *The Rise of Big Business: 1860–1920*, 3rd ed. (Hoboken, NJ: Wiley-Blackwell, 2005), and Mark Hendrickson, *American Labor and Economic Citizenship: New Capitalism from World War I to the Great Depression* (New York: Cambridge University Press, 2013).

[6] Pecklers claims that sixteen million people, or roughly one-third of the workforce, were unemployed during the worst of this period, and that number remained around ten million for the duration (Pecklers, *The Unread Vision*, 85). See also Robert McElvaine, *Down and Out in the Great Depression* (Chapel Hill: The University of North Carolina, 1983).

[7] Pecklers, *The Unread Vision*, 84–86. For another biographical view of Virgil Michel, see R. W. Franklin and Robert L. Spaeth, *Virgil Michel: American Catholic* (Collegeville, MN: Liturgical Press, 1988).

same in society, providing the raw material for forging a link between the defining characteristics of each: liturgy, on the one hand, and social justice, on the other. Such a link was forged (or, perhaps more accurately, re-forged) in United States Catholicism from the point of view of both aspects of Christian life—the liturgical and the social. Both aspects warrant some attention, which we pay here through two key figures whose work embodied each direction of linking liturgy and social justice: Virgil Michel and his liturgical theology that connected itself to social action, and Dorothy Day and her social action that connected itself to liturgy.

Virgil Michel

Virgil Michel was a Benedictine monk of Saint John's Abbey in Collegeville, Minnesota, where he founded and edited the liturgical journal *Orate Fratres* (now *Worship*), founded Liturgical Press, and taught courses in English and philosophy at Saint John's University.[8] While initially skeptical that monastic life would provide him with the ability and adequate opportunity "to study, to teach, and to promote the kingdom of God," Michel nevertheless entered the novitiate in 1909 at the age of twenty and professed his solemn vows in 1913.[9] By 1916, when he had selected the topic for his dissertation at The Catholic University of America—a study of the American thinker Orestes A. Brownson—Michel had developed an enduring conviction that justice, especially social reform, needed to be a central aim of both theology and Christian life.[10] Michel's work on Brownson further solidified this conviction and added to it a vision of ecclesiology, especially the role of the laity as "a community of apostolic faith and authority."[11] Following World War I, Michel studied both liturgy and philosophy in Louvain and Rome, and when he returned to the United States in 1926, he was "determined to pursue that harmonious relationship of liturgy and life in the Mystical Body of Christ."[12] At this point Michel was utterly entwined in the growing Liturgical Movement in the United States, so much so that he suffered a nervous breakdown and spent three years recovering (most of which time he spent living with a community of Chippewa Native

---

[8] Pecklers, *The Unread Vision*, 124.

[9] Kevin E. Schmiesing, *Within the Market Strife: American Catholic Economic Thought from* Rerum Novarum *to Vatican II* (Lanham, MD: Lexington Books, 2004), 88.

[10] Paul B. Marx, *Virgil Michel and the Liturgical Movement* (Collegeville, MN: Liturgical Press, 1957), 3–7; Pecklers, *The Unread Vision*, 124–26.

[11] Patrick Cary, quoted in Pecklers, *The Unread Vision*, 125.

[12] Pecklers, *The Unread Vision*, 126.

Americans in northern Minnesota). As Keith Pecklers argues, these three years likely provided the experiential corollary to his already-formed intellectual stance on liturgy and social reform.[13]

Michel's theology itself took as its cornerstone the concept of the Mystical Body of Christ. That said, he thought of the Mystical Body "more as a spirituality, as a way of living in society, than as a theological doctrine."[14] This fundamental aspect of Michel's thought—that its basis was in a way of *living* rather than a way of *thinking*—already points to the organic unity he saw between liturgy and social justice. Liturgy itself was for him an antidote for what had become quintessentially American individualism, a kind of lift-yourself-up-by-your-bootstraps idolization of personal economic autonomy. By constituting the liturgical community as the Mystical Body of Christ, liturgy drove home that Christians were to live within society as that Mystical Body of Christ. Such a life would be false without striving for social justice. Conversely, liturgy as the embodiment of the eschatological kingdom demanded justice within the liturgical community also—that is, within ecclesiology.[15] For Virgil Michel, liturgy emphasized the communal, just constitution of the church and was inseparable from the practice of communal action for justice in society.

Michel articulated his particular vision of social justice in this way: social justice is "that virtue by which individuals and groups contribute their positive share to the maintenance of the common good and moreover regulate all their actions in relation to the common good."[16] Such a definition emphasizes not only the aspects of both individual and collective action for justice but also the fact that social justice is an ongoing task, obligation, or habit. Social justice was not, for Michel, a structural goal to be "accomplished" but rather an ideal by which Christians are both communally and individually formed and re-formed, and therefore also an ideal toward which to strive as the Mystical Body of Christ. For Michel, while liturgy is a specifically religious practice set apart in a way from what might be called "the rest of life," liturgy nevertheless loses much of its relevance unless it connects directly *to* the practice of the rest of life (which is what the bulk of this book simply

[13] Ibid., 127–28.

[14] Ibid., 132.

[15] Ibid. A more developed study of Michel's ecclesiology can be found in Jeremy Hall, *The Full Stature of Christ: The Ecclesiology of Dom Virgil Michel* (Collegeville, MN: Liturgical Press, 1976).

[16] Virgil Michel, "Defining Social Justice," *The Commonweal* 23 (1936): 425.

calls ethics). Liturgy and the rest of life are distinct from one another in Michel's thought, but much of his thought concerns the fact that, from a Christian perspective, they cannot be separated.[17] In this way, liturgy for Michel is the formation of the Christian community as the community of social justice, the Mystical Body of Christ in the world. What better model for social justice could there be beside the model of justice, peace, and love incarnate? In Michel's words:

> It is not too much to say that the revival of true social human life will be achieved only under the inspiration of the liturgical life, since the specific divine purpose of the latter is to transform human nature after the mind of Christ and inspire it unto a life replete like His with the love of God and man.[18]

Dorothy Day

While Dorothy Day might not always be thought of as a central figure in the Liturgical Movement in the United States,[19] her commitment to drawing social activism together with liturgical participation (formal or informal) nevertheless made a significant impact on the Liturgical Movement. It is no coincidence that *The Catholic Worker*, the newspaper of social action Day edited until her death in 1980, consistently included articles dealing with liturgy generally and/or the Liturgical Movement specifically.[20] Day, drawing strength for her work from both private and public prayer,[21] was a living example of the vision of liturgy and justice that Virgil Michel heralded.

Dorothy Day was born in 1897, and her young adulthood in the first decades of the twentieth century was characterized by a commitment to justice as she saw it formed by atheist socialism.[22] Day converted to

---

[17] For example, Michel was unsure the Liturgical Movement could survive without explicitly embracing the social apostolate (Virgil Michel, "The Liturgical Movement of the Future," *America* 54 [1935]: 6–7).

[18] Virgil Michel, quoted in Pecklers, *The Unread Vision*, 135.

[19] For example, selections of her writings often focus nearly exclusively on her writings for and about social justice. See Robert Ellsberg, ed., *Dorothy Day: Selected Writings* (Maryknoll, NY: Orbis, 2002).

[20] Pecklers, *The Unread Vision*, 111.

[21] Dorothy Day, "Adventures in Prayer," in Ellsberg, *Dorothy Day*, 184.

[22] Ellsberg, *Dorothy Day*, xix–xx. For a more complete picture of Day's life, see either her autobiography, *The Long Loneliness* (New York: HarperCollins, 1997), or Jim Forest, *All Is Grace: A Biography of Dorothy Day* (Maryknoll, NY: Orbis, 2011).

Catholicism in 1927, and her commitment to justice lost none of its vigor. As Pecklers explains,

> Together with [Peter] Maurin, Day found hope in the social documents of the Church. She was convinced, like Virgil Michel and the liturgical pioneers, . . . that the key to the restoration of a Christian social order in the United States was the doctrine of the Mystical Body. Day and Maurin set out on a radical path of Christian activism, opting for a life of voluntary poverty and inviting others to join them.[23]

What began as a newspaper founded by Day and Maurin in 1933 quickly grew into the Catholic Worker network of hospitality houses aimed at providing not only food and shelter but also places where community could grow, sustained at least in part by celebration of the liturgy. The ordinariness of the liturgical elements struck a chord with Day; the messy, down-to-earth, everyday tasks and materials of the works of mercy connected to the experience of the divine not as something imported from without but as something present within, evoked by the liturgy.[24] Beyond the experience of the divine (and likely more important for Day and the Catholic Worker Movement), the liturgy was a place where the community that had been implicitly forming became explicitly united. In Day's words, speaking of the Compline liturgy celebrated in houses of the Catholic Worker, "It is the night prayer of the church, and God hears. The agnostic sings with the Catholic, because it is a communal act and he loves his brother. Our singing prepares us for another day. . . . The surroundings may be harsh, but where love is, God is."[25]

This is not to suggest that for Day the liturgy simply provided a useful mechanism to keep Catholic Worker houses docile, distracted, or artificially unified. Liturgy was an optional aspect of participating in the Catholic Worker Movement, and yet in her eyes this did not make it less vital to the movement's operation. For Day, active participation in liturgical celebration provided another place for active participation in the Catholic Worker Movement, beyond the necessary everyday tasks it required. This concept of active participation, taken from the Liturgical Movement itself and partnered with the concept of the Mystical Body of Christ, became something of a nexus between social justice and liturgy.

---

[23] Pecklers, *The Unread Vision*, 105.
[24] Ibid., 109.
[25] Dorothy Day, *Loaves and Fishes* (New York: Harper and Row, 1963), 214–15.

Liturgy and activism for social justice ultimately share the same aim, Day thought, and this was reinforced by correspondence between the Catholic Worker and Virgil Michel at *Orate Fratres*.[26] Both strive for identity and action as the Mystical Body of Christ. As Day explained, "We feel that it is very necessary to connect the liturgical movement with the social justice movement. Each one gives vitality to the other."[27]

The Catholic Worker Movement was hardly the only social or lay movement to connect its work with liturgical practice. Other groups, such as Friendship House, the Grail Movement, and the Christian Family Movement also grounded themselves in liturgy and gleaned insight from the Liturgical Movement.[28] Day's leadership with the Catholic Worker, however, and her insistence on bringing the insights of the Liturgical Movement to bear on the Catholic Worker's social justice ministry, also impacted the Liturgical Movement in a way that continually stressed the integral relationship between liturgy and justice. In a word, Dorothy Day was for the Liturgical Movement what Virgil Michel was for the Catholic Worker: a figure whose work perhaps lay in another field but nevertheless an advocate and resource whose activism was a continual reminder of their shared goals.

Liturgy and Ethics through Vatican II

In the decades leading up to the Second Vatican Council, the work of Virgil Michel and Dorothy Day inspired continued scholarship and ministry connecting liturgy and the social call of the church. Their insights and examples were given added weight by Pius XII's issuing of *Mystici Corporis Christi* in 1943, explicitly affirming the model of the Mystical Body of Christ as an apt conception of the church. While the encyclical might be argued to be at least as concerned with how hierarchy might work within the model of the Mystical Body of Christ as with the model itself, it nevertheless had the effect of validating a cornerstone of the Liturgical Movement. This provided some well-needed hierarchical warrant, because, as Pecklers points out, "As late as 1942 the doctrine [of the Mystical Body of Christ] was being attacked as a 'new conception of the Church.' "[29]

---

[26] Pecklers, *The Unread Vision*, 108–11.

[27] Mel Piehl, *Breaking Bread: The Catholic Worker and the Origin of Catholic Radicalism in America* (Philadelphia: Temple University, 1982), 84–85.

[28] See Pecklers, *The Unread Vision*, 115–24.

[29] Ibid., 32.

Mystici Corporis Christi, along with the social encyclicals *Rerum Novarum* and *Quadragesimo Anno*, provided the Liturgical Movement with something like ecclesiastical "cover," in a certain way validating and protecting those who worked within the movement and its connection to social justice from being labeled as radicals, dangerous to the church. Such was the case with Reynold Hillenbrand, under whose leadership Chicago became a vibrant center for the Liturgical Movement and social Catholicism.[30] Hillenbrand, criticizing American individualism in many of the same ways Virgil Michel had, ceaselessly emphasized the concept of the Mystical Body of Christ in his teaching, claiming both that "the world is sick of individualism and must get over it" and that "liturgy is the most complete embodiment of the beauty of the Mystical body."[31] Hillenbrand's commitment to the Liturgical Movement and social justice also led him to establish the first Summer School of Social Action for priests and, later on, another Summer School of the Liturgy. Such commitments also led him to be involved with the Grail Movement, which occasioned some trouble between him and the local bishop, ultimately leading to his removal from the seminary where he was rector. Hillenbrand was moved to a parish in Hubbard Woods, Illinois, which was transformed into a model of liturgy and social involvement; even in this move, Hillenbrand demonstrated his conviction that liturgical renewal and social action go together.[32]

While figures such as Hillenbrand drew inspiration from the social encyclicals and *Mystici Corporis Christi* as well as from examples like Virgil Michel and Dorothy Day, others, such as Hans A. Reinhold, built on the insights of the Liturgical Movement and the Catholic Worker Movement to further develop theologically what it means to connect liturgy and social ethics.[33] Reinhold's engagement with the thought of Virgil Michel and the Catholic Worker community led him to articulate a sacramental worldview springing from the idea of the Mystical Body of Christ. For

---

[30] Ibid., 145.

[31] Reynold Hillenbrand, "Address at the National Liturgical Week, Worcester, 1955," in *How Firm a Foundation: Voices of the Early Liturgical Movement*, ed. Kathleen Hughes (Chicago: Liturgy Training Publications, 1990), 134–35.

[32] Pecklers, *The Unread Vision*, 145. For an in-depth study of Hillenbrand's life and thought, see Robert Tuzik, *Reynold Hillenbrand: The Reform of the Catholic Liturgy and the Call to Social Action* (Chicago: Liturgy Training Publications, 2010).

[33] For a detailed study of Reinhold's work and thought, see Julia A. Upton, *Worship in Spirit and Truth: The Life and Legacy of H. A. Reinhold* (Collegeville, MN: Liturgical Press, 2009).

Reinhold, participation in the Body of Christ in the liturgy (particularly the sacraments) ought to carry through to participation as the Body of Christ in society. In his words, "Since we are members of that Mystical Body, which prolongs the incarnation, the state of the body social is a liturgical concern. We who claim to live by the sacraments must be found in the forefront of those who work for a new society built according to the justice and charity of Christ."[34] Reinhold was hardly the first to argue for a sacramental worldview, but his emphasis on this way of connecting sacraments and social ethics continued the trend in the United States Liturgical Movement of stressing the imperative of justice alongside liturgical and sacramental renewal.

By 1962, when the Second Vatican Council commenced (beginning with *Sacrosanctum Concilium*, largely as a result of the Liturgical Movement),[35] work on the connection between liturgy and social justice had taken many forms in the United States. Nevertheless, this was only one small part of the greater Liturgical Movement. Especially in Europe, historical scholarship on liturgical rites and practices, coupled with reforms of liturgical style and language, tended to take precedence in liturgical theology over connecting it with ethics. As H. A. Reinhold noted, "We had no Virgil Michel in Germany. The close inter-connection of the liturgical revival with social reform . . . was never expressed in that forceful way in which you see it in the writings of the late Dom Virgil and *Orate Fratres*."[36] This lack of emphasis on what had been a hallmark of the Liturgical Movement in the United States persevered into the promulgation of *Sacrosanctum Concilium* in 1963, which, while it did speak briefly of the Eucharist as a "bond of charity"[37] and mentions in passing the sacraments' purpose to dispose the faithful to the practice of charity,[38] largely leaves the connection between liturgy and justice untouched. Other documents of Vatican II do attend in certain ways to this connection—for example, *Apostolicam Actuositatem* in 1965—but the language of the *Sacrosanctum Concilium* omits terms such as "justice," "ethics," and "morality."[39]

---

[34] H. A. Reinhold, "A Social Leaven?," *Orate Fratres* 25 (1951): 518.

[35] Frank C. Senn, *Christian Liturgy* (Minneapolis, MN: Fortress, 1997), 629.

[36] Marx, *Virgil Michel*, 180.

[37] Vatican Council II, *Sacrosanctum Concilium: The Constitution on the Sacred Liturgy*, para. 47.

[38] Ibid., para. 59.

[39] One of the reasons for this was likely that the American bishops were rather silent during the first session of Vatican II, though even had they not been, it would

Strikingly, while the connection between liturgy and social justice tended to remain a distinctive mark of the Liturgical Movement in the United States as opposed to in Europe (at least until after Vatican II), it also tended to be missed by Protestant appropriations of the Liturgical Movement in the United States. For example, twentieth-century Lutheranism in the United States was certainly indebted to the Liturgical Movement in its reemphasis on aspects like frequent reception of Holy Communion, the active participation of the laity, and the communal nature of the sacraments, but studies of this impact of the Liturgical Movement rarely mention either Virgil Michel or the connection to social justice and ethics.[40] In the years leading up to the turn of the twenty-first century, however, a number of theologians, Roman Catholic and Protestant, have returned to the connection of liturgy and justice, or liturgy and ethics, as both a theological tenet and a theological conclusion. Louis-Marie Chauvet is one major example of this return, but some snapshots of other figures are warranted in order to situate this discussion of sacraments and ethics in its correct theological context.

Contemporary Directions in Liturgy and Ethics

In the decades following the Second Vatican Council, many areas of theology underwent explosions of scholarly study and creativity similar to that which liturgical theology had in the early twentieth century. The development of contextual theologies, engagement with late-modern and postmodern philosophies, dialogue with the insights of postcolonial theories, and the massive technological advancement of recent years have all provided theology a rich milieu in which to develop.[41] In this

---

be mere speculation to guess whether justice would have entered the conversation. For a detailed account of the first session of the council, see Xavier Rynn, *Vatican Council II* (Maryknoll, NY: Orbis, 1999), 1–134.

[40] See, for example, Timothy C. J. Quill, *The Impact of the Liturgical Movement on American Lutheranism* (Lanham, MD: The Scarecrow Press, 1997), or Frank C. Senn, *Christian Liturgy*, 609–71.

[41] For a description of contextual theology, see Stephen B. Bevans, *Models of Contextual Theology* (Maryknoll, NY: Orbis, 1992). The work of scholars such as Jacques Derrida, Michel de Certeau, and Gayatri Chakravorty Spivak embody representative postmodern and postcolonial theorization. See Jacques Derrida, *Writing and Difference*, trans. Alan Bass (London: Routledge, 1978), Michel de Certeau, *The Practice of Everyday Life*, trans. Steven F. Rendall (Berkeley: University of California, 1988), and Gayatri Chakravorty Spivak, *An Aesthetic Education in the Era of Globalization* (Cambridge, MA: Harvard University, 2013). Thinkers such as Jean-Luc Marion (see his

theological context, inquiry into the relationship between liturgy and ethics has often been subsumed as a part of a thinker's larger project. As such, what follows are brief descriptions of three theologians whose scholarship will serve to gesture toward what work is currently being done in liturgy and ethics, thus locating this project within the discipline. The discussion begins with the theology of Don E. Saliers, whose work in liturgical theology has stressed aesthetics and affections and thereby works toward ethics. A summary of J.-M.-R. Tillard follows, whose ecclesiological work draws on and impacts liturgical theology. Finally, the discussion will close with the thought of Bruce Morrill, who has worked at the nexus of liturgical theology and political theology.

Don E. Saliers

Don E. Saliers, an American Methodist theologian, has written extensively on Christian worship and human affections, senses, and aesthetics.[42] His work rarely proceeds, however, without attending to the ethical implications of his theological reflections. For Saliers, there is an "internal, conceptual link between liturgy and ethics,"[43] which springs from the law of belief (lex credendi) and the law of prayer (*lex orandi*)—a

---

Being Given: Toward a Phenomenology of Givenness, trans. Jeffrey Kosky [Redwood City, CA: Stanford University, 2002], or *God without Being*, trans. Thomas A. Carlson [Chicago: University of Chicago, 1991]), along with volumes such as *Decolonizing the Body of Christ: Theology and Theory after Empire?* (David Joy and Joseph Duggan, eds. [New York: Palgrave Macmillan, 2012]), have worked to engage with these theories from a Christian and/or theological perspective. For theological engagement of the massive advancement of technology, see Noreen Herzfeld, *Technology and Religion: Remaining Human in a Co-Created World* (West Conshohocken, PA: Templeton, 2009), Brent Walters, *From Human to Posthuman: Christian Theology and Technology in a Postmodern World* (Burlington, VT: Ashgate, 2006), or the essays in Nancy Murphy and Christopher C. Knight, eds., *Human Identity at the Intersection of Science, Technology, and Religion* (Burlington, VT: Ashgate, 2010).

[42] See, for example, Don E. Saliers, *Worship Come to Its Senses* (Nashville, TN: Abingdon, 1996), Don E. Saliers, *The Soul in Paraphrase: Prayer and the Religious Affections* (Memphis, TN: Order of Saint Luke, 1991), or Don Saliers and Emily Saliers, *A Song to Sing, A Life to Live: Reflections on Music as Spiritual Practice* (San Francisco, CA: Jossey-Bass, 2005).

[43] Don E. Saliers, "Liturgy and Ethics: Some New Beginnings," in *Liturgy and the Moral Self: Humanity at Full Stretch Before God*, ed. E. Byron Anderson and Bruce T. Morrill (Collegeville, MN: Liturgical Press, 1998), 16.

link he terms the law of ethical action, the *lex agendi*.[44] For Saliers, liturgy is multivalent; it serves to accomplish many things, one of the foremost being ethical formation. Saliers, however, takes a slightly different approach than his forebears in the Liturgical Movement. Rather than focusing on the concept of the Mystical Body of Christ and a sacramental worldview (though these things can certainly be found in his thought), he argues that liturgy forms Christians for ethics affectively or, in a certain sense, aesthetically:

> The relationships between liturgy and ethics are most adequately formulated by specifying how certain affections and virtues are formed and expressed in the modalities of communal prayer and ritual action. These modalities of prayer enter into the formation of the self in community.[45]

Liturgy for Saliers, then, is a kind of group affective formation for ethical life. Such formation takes place, however, not simply as a human community forming its members on its own but rather as a human community being formed in worshiping relationship with God. Such a point might appear to go without saying, but the significance of this relationship with the divine for Saliers makes liturgy not simply affective and formative but also eschatological.[46] While Saliers's conception of liturgical eschatology is not as "realized" as that of some other contemporary theologians,[47] he is convinced that eschatology is inseparable from liturgical theology. If liturgy forms the community, the model for formation is the Kingdom of God. This means that Christian worship, focused as it is (and ought to be) on recalling and reflecting on the past events of salvation history, also participates in salvation history by looking forward to the final times and making them present. As Saliers notes, speaking of Christian Advent liturgies, "Are we to ponder the coming

---

[44] E. Byron Anderson and Bruce T. Morrill, "Introduction," in *Liturgy and the Moral Self*, 6.

[45] Saliers, "Liturgy and Ethics: Some New Beginnings," 17.

[46] Don E. Saliers, *Worship as Theology: Foretaste of Glory Divine* (Nashville, TN: Abingdon, 1994), 14.

[47] See, for example, John Zizioulas's view of the eucharistic community as "*exactly the same as*" the universal church gathered around Christ (John D. Zizioulas, *Being as Communion* [Crestwood, NY: St. Vladimir's Seminary, 1985], 149), which, in Paul McPartlan's view, is "the future, eschatological assembly" (Paul McPartlan, *The Eucharist Makes the Church* [Fairfax, VA: Eastern Christian Publications, 2006], 169).

of Jesus in Bethlehem, or are we to look for his final victory over sin and death? The answer is yes to *both* questions."[48]

Beyond the eschatological character of Christian worship, Saliers argues that liturgy itself ought to be normative for Christian life and theology, particularly ethics. He acknowledges that theology *can* be done without consideration for liturgy, but doing so loses something essential to Christianity. In Saliers's words, "Christian ethics and the shape of the moral life cannot be adequately understood apart from how Christians actually worship God."[49] The reason for this is that ethics for Saliers exists not as a set of rules in a vacuum but rather as actions lived out in relationship *with* God and community. As such, it is the location of the encounter with God and community—liturgy—that provides the quintessential opportunity for ethical formation and subsequent reflection. This activity of connecting liturgy and ethics for Saliers is an affective one; it operates on the level of human senses and emotions, and only subsequently on conscious reflection. As a result, liturgical art, style, and location for Saliers play essential roles for Christian worship in the service of what are more commonly thought of as liturgical elements: scripture, bread, wine, preaching, etc. Liturgy is an encounter with the divine and with one another, and such an encounter cannot help but be influenced and formed by the circumstances that surround and embody it.

One might think of the way Saliers connects liturgy and ethics as that of liturgy inspiring ethics, or liturgy translating the ethical call aesthetically. Such a formulation would be a way of naming grace for him: bringing Christians to encounter the kingdom of God they find in the gospel and drawing them into the challenge to embody that kingdom. In his words, "Authentic liturgy lures us by grace into a new pathos, now directed to the passion of God at the heart of the gospel."[50] This being the case, it is worth noting that Saliers maintains there is a multiplicity of connections between liturgy and ethics, or at least as many ways of connecting them as there are human affections. As Saliers argues, "we must admit that it is misleading to speak of *the* relation between liturgy and ethics as though there were only one essential linkage. There is a multitude of linkages between liturgy . . . and the lived narratives of

---

[48] Saliers, *Worship as Theology*, 220. Emphasis in original.
[49] Ibid., 172.
[50] Ibid., 38.

our lives."[51] For Saliers, liturgy is not only eschatological but also ethically formative in ways specific to the particular Christian encounters it facilitates. Liturgy and ethics cannot be separated from each other, but the links between them through affections and aesthetics are as varied as the contexts and communities in which they are practiced.

J.-M.-R. Tillard

The work of Canadian Dominican theologian Jean-Marie Roger Tillard is primarily ecclesiological, but the principal direction of his ecclesiology—that of communion ecclesiology—both finds its base on liturgical and ethical foundations and brings with it liturgical and ethical implications. For example, Tillard's work *Flesh of the Church, Flesh of Christ: At the Source of the Ecclesiology of Communion* is an attempt to locate in the scriptures and the early church the basis for the church as communion. In that endeavor, however, Tillard relies at least partly on the organic unity of the community of faith, the celebrations of that community, and the ethical concerns of those in the community. In his words, "Confession of faith, liturgical worship, and concrete concern about others necessarily go together."[52] Tillard's focus is not necessarily to tease out the liturgical or ethical implications his chosen theological bases provide, but his work is nevertheless pregnant with them.

The overarching concept that provides the structure for much of Tillard's work is undoubtedly the concept of communion.[53] The very basis of Christian life, Tillard argues, is relationship with others (and God), and the Christian model of right relationship is communion. Much could be said about how Tillard conceives of communion, but for our purposes, two integral aspects of communion stand out: communion is ethical, and communion is liturgical. Both of these aspects mean that for Tillard communion cannot be conceived of merely as a state; communion contains within its very core the actions of those who share it. In Tillard's words, "If we needed to characterize in one word the fundamental inspiration of Christian behavior, we would speak of communion—communion with God and others in faith, charity, and hope."[54]

---

[51] Ibid., 187.

[52] J.-M.-R. Tillard, *Flesh of the Church, Flesh of Christ: At the Source of the Ecclesiology of Communion* (Collegeville, MN: Liturgical Press, 2001), 18.

[53] See, for example, J.-M.-R. Tillard, *Church of Churches: The Ecclesiology of Communion* (Collegeville, MN: Liturgical Press, 1980).

[54] Tillard, *Flesh of the Church*, 1.

Beyond connoting superficial getting-along-with persons or groups of people who claim the name Christian, communion for Tillard is bound up with the actions of those persons and communities. This is to say that, for Tillard, communion has as much a horizontal dimension as a vertical one. The communion of Christ (which is Christian communion, the communion of the church) has an ethical dimension, because, as Tillard states, "Where the communion of Christ Jesus is not present, the Christian way of being is absent. . . . This relation to Christ is inseparable from the relation to others. The other implies others."[55]

Beyond its ethical dimension for Tillard, Christian communion also has a necessary liturgical dimension. Communion in Tillard's thought is never simply human community; it is communion with Christ, and that basis undergirds all forms of Christian communion. In this light, the liturgical dimension of communion is constitutive; it is in the liturgy (primarily in the Eucharist) that Christians renew and celebrate communion with Christ and one another. This is, for Tillard, like the ethical dimension of communion, inseparable from communion as a concept: "The Eucharist is explained by the Church, the Church is explained by the Eucharist."[56]

In Tillard's thought, the connection between liturgy and ethics is not the primary focus, but it does not need to be in order for his thought to be informative of current directions of work on the subject. Tillard's primary focus—communion, especially in the context of ecclesiology—rests on a foundation of both liturgy and ethics. There are certainly other aspects of Tillard's thought concerning communion, but liturgy and ethics remain constitutive for him. Neither the ethical dimension nor the liturgical dimension can stand on its own as the background for communion, and neither is communion self-reliant; it requires the other two. Tillard's work, ecclesiological as it is, builds on and impacts liturgical theology and ethics.

Bruce Morrill

American Jesuit Bruce Morrill's principal work in liturgy and ethics appears in his book *Anamnesis as Dangerous Memory,* in which he draws figures from both political and liturgical theology into conversation. Primarily using the work of Johann Baptist Metz and Alexander Schmemann, Morrill provides an example of ways in which theologians whose

---

[55] Ibid., 3–4.
[56] Ibid., 28.

fields do not necessarily cross can be used to enrich one another's thought. Morrill's main objective in *Anamnesis as Dangerous Memory* is not simply to show *that* liturgy and ethics (or politics) are connected but rather to additionally tease out liturgical and ethical implications via a conversation between theologians whose work has already demonstrated that connection. The "pressing question," Morrill maintains, is "whether and to what extent the liturgy is able to shape the life of the Church and its mission in the modern world."[57]

The fundamental points Morrill draws from Metz are the interdependence of mysticism (liturgy) and politics (ethics), on the one hand, and their distinct integrities, on the other.[58] For Metz, mystical practices are goods in themselves, insofar as "profound human freedom (so greatly inhibited in late-modern culture and society) is experienced when believers give themselves over to the narrative and symbolic world of the sacramental liturgy."[59] The role of liturgy is in this way, for Metz, "not simply an instrumental one in relation to ethics and politics,"[60] but liturgy does embody a kind of ethical and political urgency because of its eschatological emphasis. Christian liturgy contains within it both a remembering of the past and an expectant anticipation of the future, specifically the future end of days and coming of God's reign. As Morrill explains, "For Metz, the purpose of immanent expectation of the parousia, belief in a definite end of time, prevents Christian faith (the practice of imitating Christ) from succumbing to resignation and apathy."[61] Christian liturgy is *both* valuable in itself *and* instrumental for the imitation of Christ, i.e., Christian ethical living.

Conversely, the *imitatio Christi* (which for Metz seems to capture the goal of Christian ethical and political life) is both a good in itself and an aid to the Christian experience of liturgy. On the one hand, Christian faith is itself for Metz the practical imitation of Christ; it is "about a life lived with interest in the suffering of others, for which the apocalypse will be the definitive revelation of the God of Jesus as the God of the living and the dead."[62] *Imitatio Christi* is, for Metz, what Christian life ought to look like. The imitation of Christ also feeds into liturgical

---

[57] Bruce Morrill, *Anamnesis as Dangerous Memory: Political and Liturgical Theology in Dialogue* (Collegeville, MN: Liturgical Press, 2000), 19.

[58] Ibid., 190–91.

[59] Ibid., 190.

[60] Ibid.

[61] Ibid., 199.

[62] Ibid., 189.

practice, however, because it is those who imitate Christ—specifically Christ's mercy—that in turn recognize Christ more clearly in liturgical celebrations. As Morrill explains it, "The mercy at the heart of the Gospel which Christians receive, at the heart of God whom they confess at baptism, at the heart of Jesus whom they commemorate at the Eucharist, is only genuinely *known* by those who *act* mercifully in history and society."[63] Christian ethics and political action—the *imitatio Christi*—are themselves both goals of Christian faith and aids to Christian liturgy.

Morrill draws on Schmemann as a dialogue partner for Metz mainly because of Schmemann's way of conceiving of liturgy and Christian knowledge. As Morrill says, "In [Schmemann's] own work he explicitly argued for the practice of liturgy as a privileged form of knowing, indeed, the fundamental way in which believers know and appropriate the content of faith."[64] For Schmemann, liturgical practice is paradigmatic for the Christian worldview, a claim that can be read as nearly the inverse of Metz's concept of the importance of mysticism for politics. While Schmemann argues for liturgical practice as a primary way of Christian knowing, Metz points out that true knowledge in the liturgy depends at least in part on the imitation of Christ outside the practice of liturgy. Morrill does not play these two views against one another, but sees them as mutually enriching; in both views, Christian life in the world and Christian life in liturgy are inextricably linked.

One other field in which Morrill sees a possibility for discussion between these two figures is eschatology. While Metz emphasizes the liturgical anticipation of the parousia, for Schmemann the liturgy itself *is* a moment of the parousia breaking into history.[65] For Metz, the liturgy has an apocalyptic character; for Schmemann, the liturgy has a character of realized eschatology. Metz's concern is that liturgy energizes the Christian community for political and ethical action, but in what might be seen as a complementary way, Schmemann conceives of the liturgy *not* as anticipating a future political or ethical moment toward which humans ought to strive but rather as an experience *of* that future mo-

---

[63] Ibid., 203. Morrill's insight into the liturgical life of Christianity continues in others of his works, notably his contributions to *Bodies of Worship: Explorations in Theory and Practice* (Collegeville, MN: Liturgical Press, 2000), and his works *Divine Worship and Human Healing: Liturgical Theology at the Margins of Life and Death* (Collegeville, MN: Liturgical Press, 2009), and *Encountering Christ in the Eucharist: The Paschal Mystery in People, Word, and Sacrament* (New York: Paulist Press, 2012).

[64] Morrill, *Anamnesis as Dangerous Memory*, 191.

[65] Ibid., 192.

ment in the present. The effects may be quite similar, but the models remain distinct.

The goal of Morrill's project is not simply to juxtapose two theologians; he additionally wishes to draw implications from this discussion for the liturgical and ethical life of the church. (This method mirrors some of the goals of this book.) Two of the implications he names bear mention here: first, the interplay of liturgy and ethics (or mysticism and politics) provides a source for ecclesial renewal that neither field could provide on its own. Political action itself is not enough to reinvigorate the life of the church, and neither is liturgical celebration on its own. As Morrill points out, borrowing from Metz, "Only if believers are engaged in the dialectical praxis of mysticism and politics can they experience the faith as an ongoing hunger and urgent desire for the just and loving God revealed in the person and gospel of Jesus."[66] Second, the interplay of liturgy and ethics is multilayered. Christian ethics and political action take many forms, and not every form can resonate with a liturgical practice. Likewise, Christian liturgical practices are not interchangeable, so one ought not to expect everything that is required for ecclesial renewal to spring forth from just one or a few of them. For Morrill, liturgy is connected to ethics and politics, but it is not a silver bullet.

Background: Louis-Marie Chauvet

Louis-Marie Chauvet is a French Catholic priest, currently employed as a pastor in the Diocese of Pontoise. Born in 1942, Chauvet was ordained a priest in 1966 and was a professor at L'Institut Catholique de Paris until he took up his current ministry.[67] While his major scholarly works include but three volumes and a host of articles, he has gained considerable influence in liturgical and sacramental theology in the United States, at least in part because of the organic unity his theology maintains between sacraments and ethics.[68] Chauvet's theological background and conversation partners will be explained in greater detail in chapter 3 below, but in order to situate that discussion, an understanding

---

[66] Ibid., 211–12.

[67] Joseph John Fortuna, *Two Approaches to Language in Sacramental Efficacy Compared: Thomas Aquinas in the* Summa Theologiae *and Louis-Marie Chauvet*, (PhD diss., The Catholic University of America, 1989), 3–4.

[68] Such a unity meshes easily with the scholarship that springs from the Liturgical Movement in the United States, with its emphasis on liturgy and social justice.

of his philosophical influences is warranted. What follows is a summary of three philosophical figures on whose insights Chauvet's theology relies. First, Martin Heidegger provides the background for Chauvet's resistance to metaphysics, his conception of language, his suspicion of immediacy, and the ways he conceives of presence and absence. Second, the philosopher/anthropologist Marcel Mauss is the primary source for Chauvet's concept of symbolic exchange and the gift. Finally, Jacques Derrida, as a philosophical contemporary of Chauvet, represents a counterpoint to developing the concept of the gift and symbolic exchange after Mauss. As such, Derrida's work serves to throw Chauvet's insights into sharper relief.

Martin Heidegger

Martin Heidegger provides a good deal of the philosophical foundation for Chauvet's project. Chauvet's suspicion of classical metaphysics and its operation in theology is heavily indebted to Heidegger's critique of metaphysics, as is his understanding of language, mediation, and the concepts of presence and absence.

Heidegger's critique of metaphysics takes as its major thrust the conviction that the Western philosophical tradition (that is to say, philosophy based in metaphysics from the thought of the Ancient Greeks onward) has forgotten the essential difference between Being and beings. Beings (*Seinde*) are for Heidegger simply objects, or "things that are."[69] This is not Heidegger's problem, as objects have always been part of the stuff of philosophy. What a thing is in itself, what it is accidentally, or how it appears have all been questions that, from early on, humans have asked concerning both themselves and the realities that have surrounded them.

Heidegger's trouble begins when speaking about Being itself (*Sein*) rather than beings.[70] If beings are objects that can be said to exist, then metaphysics has tended to treat Being like another noun, namely, the "stuff" that is common to all beings.[71] To be fair, Heidegger acknowledges that metaphysical reflection on Being has been somewhat distinct

---

[69] Glenn P. Ambrose, *The Theology of Louis-Marie Chauvet: Overcoming Onto-Theology with the Sacramental Tradition* (Surrey, England: Ashgate, 2012), 11.

[70] See Richard Polt, *Heidegger: An Introduction* (Ithaca, NY: Cornell, 1999), 23–27.

[71] Louis-Marie Chauvet, *Symbol and Sacrament*, (Collegeville, MN: Liturgical Press, 1995), 26.

from reflection on beings. Beings are finite or limited, while Being may not be. Beings can be both causes and effects, while Being only causes. To be blunt, metaphysics throughout the Western tradition has tended to maintain that Being is, for lack of a better explanation, the "ground and cause" of all beings.[72] Heidegger's critique of this conception of Being is not that he has an alternative and/or better way to describe Being but rather that the very grammar by which such formulations approach Being already betrays an assumption of the essential identity between Being and beings.[73] Beings *are* objects that appear as given. Being *is* the ground/cause of all beings. These two sentences describe two different things (Being and beings), but they remain *things*, that is, Being has been reduced to the order of beings. This problem presents itself any time one attempts to explain what Being *is*. Whenever one may begin a sentence with "Being *is* (fill in the blank)," one has already begun with the assumption that Being is a kind of stuff, *something* that can be used as the subject of a sentence. For Heidegger, this is the mistake of metaphysics. One ought not to think of Being as the subject of a sentence; instead, one ought to think of Being more as a verb. In Glenn P. Ambrose's words, "*Sein* is more an event or process by which *Seinde* are made manifest."[74]

This conception of Being as more like a process or activity than like a kind of stuff or ground carries ramifications beyond simply how we might think of what *is*. *How* we think of what is—or rather, how we formulate thoughts at all—is also linked to Heidegger's critique of metaphysics. This, for Heidegger, is the issue of language, namely, the issue of whether language is a tool used by humans to express thoughts that are prelinguistic, or whether language is intrinsic to the process of thought itself. With the same move that we will see Chauvet make in chapter 3, Heidegger's stance is that language is not instrumental but constitutive of human existence. Speaking from the human point of view, "language is the house of being."[75]

---

[72] Ambrose, *The Theology of Louis-Marie Chauvet*, 12. See also Martin Heidegger, *Introduction to Metaphysics*, trans. Gregory Fried and Richard Polt (New Haven: Yale University, 2000), 79–97.

[73] Heidegger, *Introduction to Metaphysics*, 55–78.

[74] Ambrose, *The Theology of Louis-Marie Chauvet*, 11.

[75] Martin Heidegger, "Letter on Humanism," in *Basic Writings: Martin Heidegger*, ed. David Krell (New York: HarperCollins, 1993), 217. For Heidegger himself on language, see his *On the Way to Language* (New York: Harper & Row, 1982), or his

All this makes for a reality that can be experienced only as mediated, but the question might be asked: if Being is more a verb than a noun, that is, something that beings *do* (or perhaps something that is done to them) rather than something that lurks behind or under beings, what sort of mediation could there possibly be between Being and beings? They might seem to be *immediately* connected. Heidegger insists, however, that there can be no immediacy of beings to Being; to understand his reservations, one must appreciate Heidegger's notions of presence and absence in relation to Being and language.

For Heidegger, immediacy between a being and Being (or even between a being and itself, or between beings) is illusory because at its base such a concept is subject to critiques analogous to his critique of the metaphysical tradition more generally speaking. To assume immediacy between a being and Being has already fallen into the trap of speaking of Being as an entity.[76] Further, even if Being is spoken of as a verb, to speak of immediacy between a being and its Being still domesticates the concept of Being; it suddenly is something to which we have unconditional access, and the concept is drained of its essential mystery.

Instead of immediate presence of Being to beings, Heidegger maintains that Being's presence is always characterized by a certain absence, or a withdrawal of Being from beings. One might envision such a withdrawal, or the component of absence within presence, in relation to a being normally conceived of as present-at-hand. Heidegger uses the example of a cabinetmaker and the wood he or she uses as part of the craft.[77] On a surface level, the cabinetmaker uses the wood to create his or her wares. For a cabinetmaker who is truly proficient in the craft, however, there is an element of the wood that retreats from the maker's gaze. The cabinetmaker does not necessarily approach the wood and dictate what is to be made and how; instead, he or she to a certain extent discovers what the wood can do and is sensitive to the potential hidden in each piece. The wood, inanimate in every respect as long as one approaches it in everydayness, takes on a life—where did it come from, what can it do, how can it best be worked to show forth its cur-

---

Poetry, Language, Thought (New York: HarperCollins, 2001). For a somewhat more digestible explanation, see Jeffrey Powell, *Heidegger and Language* (Bloomington: Indiana University, 2013).

[76] Heidegger, *Introduction to Metaphysics*, 55–78.

[77] Martin Heidegger, "What Calls for Thinking?," in Krell, *Basic Writings*, 379.

rently veiled beauty? These and other considerations constitute a kind of dialogue between the cabinetmaker and his or her materials: they are no longer present-at-hand; they are present, but they also retreat into absence.[78]

Analogously, Being itself is present to beings, but only by also withdrawing into absence in the very act of its presence. This is the point of mediation and the nexus of Being and language. In Ambrose's words, "Language, like Being, is akin to a living presence which arrives and withdraws. It is an announcing and a letting-come forth."[79] Just as humans' usual experience of the world is prone to sinking into everydayness, so humans' usual experience of language is that of the everyday, one-dimensional, present-at-hand tools for the expression of thoughts. Again like Being, however, language in its more full (or correct) sense is not simply a tool employed by humans; it is, rather, an activity that makes humans who and what they are. Humans may experience language as a given—as a set of instruments to be worked with until one obtains some desired result—but while language is this in some sense, it is also more than this. In the same way that the skilled cabinetmaker both uses wood and tools and discovers in the wood and tools a reality that retreats beyond his or her gaze, the person skilled with language (for Heidegger, the poet) both uses words and phrases and discovers in them the presence of a certain absence—a fullness of meaning that one cannot immediately grasp. Language expresses reality, but it also veils it.[80]

All this means that when conceiving of beings, Being, and language, the world is, for Heidegger, far deeper than our everyday experience of it. Heidegger's response to this everydayness is not, however, an active seeking for the reality hidden under our world and words. Such a response would be to strive again for immediacy, to attempt again to reduce Being and language to the level of everydayness. Instead, Heidegger describes an approach to reality he calls *Gelassenheit*. Huston Smith summarizes the concept succinctly: *Gelassenheit* is a "reverent, choiceless letting-be of what is in order that it may reveal itself in the essence of its being."[81] Notice that this has both an active and a passive component:

[78] Ibid., 374–80.

[79] Ambrose, *The Theology of Louis-Marie Chauvet*, 18.

[80] See Heidegger, *Poetry, Language, Thought*.

[81] Huston Smith, *Beyond the Post-Modern Mind* (Wheaton, IL: The Theosophical Publishing House, 1982), 87.

active because one ought to *let* what is simply *be*, and passive in that what *is* reveals itself—it is not apprehended as if such a thing were a task. *Gelassenheit* does not obliterate everydayness; it operates within our everyday world as a sort of stance or attitude, a consent to the fact that our reality is more than simply its surface level.[82] *Gelassenheit* acknowledges that our world is experienced as everyday and yet consents to the mediation of deeper, more profound reality by the very language or beings we experience in everydayness.

Marcel Mauss

Most of the philosophical background Chauvet draws outside of Heidegger is found in recent discussions of the philosophy of the gift. In this regard, Marcel Mauss's 1950 work *Essai sur le Don* is seminal. The essay is essentially a study of traditions and customs of gift giving kept by non-modernized or ancient peoples (the subtitle of the work is, tellingly, *The Form and Reason for Exchange in Archaic Societies*),[83] but in it Mauss points out perhaps *the* main issue that quickly became the chief subject of discussion in philosophies of the gift.

Mauss's main insight is that gift giving, in basically every society he studies, has both a voluntary and obligatory aspect. He makes this explicit when he explores the tradition of the potlatch in the American Northwest; there is an obligation to give, to receive, and to reciprocate. In very brief summary: according to Native American custom, the potlatch is an event or gathering in which gifts are exchanged. The essence of the event is that some person in a position of honor and wealth, demonstrating that such honor and wealth is deserved, gives a lavish party and distributes gifts copiously to the visitors. This could be on the occasion of a wedding, a funeral, or a "summit" of sorts with other groups or tribes, but the main thrust of the event is the excessive consumption and giving away of goods. Mauss relies on Davy in describing four distinct kinds of the potlatch, but he maintains that in terms of gift, reception, and reciprocation, they are "comparatively identical."[84] Mauss's point in this study is that the concept of the gift supports entire

---

[82] Timothy M Brunk, *Liturgy and Life: The Unity of Sacraments and Ethics in the Theology of Louis-Marie Chauvet* (New York: Peter Lang, 2007), 105.

[83] Marcel Mauss, *The Gift: The Form and Reason for Exchange in Archaic Societies*, trans. W. D. Halls (New York: W. W. Norton, 1990).

[84] Ibid., 38–39.

systems of economy that exist apart from our current conception of the market or money economy.[85] There is certainly obligation in the gift economy, but it does not unfold in the same way the market economy does—more changes hands than just money. Exactly *what* changes hands in addition to money is something Mauss only hints at, but this point is the beginning of late-modern discussion of the gift. The insight that it is more than goods that changes hands in gift giving provides the basis for further, more philosophical reflection on the gift—both in Chauvet and his contemporaries.

Jacques Derrida[86]

Moving forward from Mauss, perhaps the most influential philosopher on the subject of the gift has been Jacques Derrida.[87] While Chauvet does not cite him extensively on the subject of the gift, Derrida's contributions do frame a good portion of the conversation of which Chauvet is a part, and he provides an illustrative counterpoint to Chauvet that will help throw Chauvet's insights into sharper relief. For Derrida, the gift is what he terms "the impossible."[88] *Giving* is not necessarily impossible (though it is only in light of death that giving and taking are really possible for Derrida),[89] but giving a/the *gift* is the

---

[85] Ibid., 3–4.

[86] Much of this section on Derrida (pp. 25–29) is adapted from another article of mine that appeared as "Symbolic Exchange and the Gift: Louis-Marie Chauvet and Jacques Derrida in Dialogue," *Obsulta* 4 (2011).

[87] One ought to note, however, that the late modern period has seen multiple philosophical and theological reflections on and theories of the gift. For theological approaches, see Jean-Luc Marion's *Being Given*, as well as John Milbank, *Being Reconciled* (London: Routledge, 2003) and Antonio López, *Gift and the Unity of Being* (Eugene, OR: Wipf & Stock, 2013). For philosophical approaches to the gift beyond Derrida, see Eric R. Severson, ed., *Gift and Economy: Ethics, Hospitality and the Market* (Newcastle upon Tyne, UK: Cambridge Scholars, 2012), or Paul Ricoeur, *Memory, History, Forgetting*, trans. Kathleen Blamey and David Pellauer (Chicago: University of Chicago, 2006), 479–86. An interesting conversation between Derrida and Marion on the gift can be found in John D. Caputo and Michael J. Scanlon, eds., *God, the Gift, and Postmodernism* (Bloomington: Indiana University, 1999).

[88] Jacques Derrida, *Given Time: I. Counterfeit Money*, trans. Peggy Kamuf (Chicago: University of Chicago Press, 1992), 7.

[89] Jacques Derrida, *The Gift of Death and Literature in Secret*, 2nd ed., trans. David Wills (Chicago: University of Chicago Press, 2008), 45. The relation of the gift to death is a worthy topic in order to completely understand where Derrida is coming

impossible. As such for Derrida, one cannot speak discursively of the gift; it is an enigma.

Note that Derrida does not claim the gift is impossible as an act. He claims instead that as a concept, the gift is *the* impossible. This distinction may seem slight, but understanding what Derrida means in this regard helps clarify (relatively speaking) the rest of what he does with the gift. As an example, there are certain things in the world that are impossible: palm trees do not grow in the tundra, it is impossible to see amoebas without a microscope, and people will never be wholly satisfied with whatever the current tax rate is. A specific type of impossibility characterizes these impossible things, however: they are impossible because some element in them is left wanting. Palm trees want for hardiness; if they could survive colder temperatures, perhaps they could indeed grow in the tundra. The human eye wants for keenness; if it were a good deal keener, we might be able to see amoebas without using microscopes. And, of course, if taxes were just and humans were patient and charitable, perhaps everyone could indeed be satisfied with the rate of levy.

In each of these situations, want precipitates impossibility. Nevertheless, one could imagine a world in which these things would not be impossible. The issues are *derivatively* impossible (my word, not Derrida's); if circumstances were different, they might in fact be achievable. This is qualitatively different from the impossibility Derrida ascribes to the gift. For Derrida, the gift is *the* impossible, that is, the essence of what makes a gift also makes it impossible. This might be called *intrinsic* impossibility (again, not Derrida's word), and it also has its members: round squares, hot ice, vegetarian veal, and other things that border on the absurd. Absurdity is the direction in which Derrida takes his thought on the gift. *As gift*, the gift is impossibility. Its impossibility does not derive from anything lacking about the concept, the material, or the performance. Rather, it is the impossible precisely because those things that constitute it are—as a set—impossible. Neither is this due to some imperfection of gift giving; it is exactly the *purity* of the gift—the necessary purity for Derrida—that utterly separates it from the realm of the possible.

---

from with the concept of the gift. This discussion limits itself, however, to a brief outline of Derrida's vision, and so will draw almost exclusively from his work *Given Time* rather than *The Gift of Death*.

The constitution of the gift in Derrida, that is, the essential elements that precipitate the gift's impossibility, might be thought of as threefold: (1) the structure of the gift, (2) the character of the gift, and (3) the matter of the gift.[90] The first constitutive element of the gift, that of its structure, Derrida explains as deriving basically from convention: "some 'one' intends to give or gives 'something' to 'someone other.' "[91] For the gift to be a gift, there ought to be a giver, a gift, and a receiver; absence of any of these three components causes the gift to present itself to us as incomplete.[92] Derrida points out that this structure in the end amounts to a tautology; if we try to explain what the structure of the gift is, we immediately assume that our audience already has some "precomprehension" of the gift. In his words, when I define the gift's structure, "I suppose that I know and that you know what 'to give,' 'gift,' 'donor,' 'donee' mean in our common language."[93] This is the first constituent and also the first trouble with the gift—any attempt to apprehend its structure of giver-gift-receiver presupposes its definition in the explanation—but this does not, on its own, make the gift the impossible (this point requires the other two also to do that).

The second constitutive element of the gift, its character, is what ought to separate it from an economic exchange of goods or services: the gift must be gratuitous. As Derrida articulates, "For there to be a gift, there must be no reciprocity, return, exchange, counterfeit, or debt."[94] In essence, the gift must be free, in all senses of the term. On a certain level this character of the gift would be obvious, but Derrida takes a very hard stance on the purity of the gift's gratuitousness. For him, *any* reciprocity for a gift given is tantamount to repayment (which nullifies the gift), *any* satisfaction or even giving intention on the part of the giver is the same as reimbursement (also nullifying the gift), and even any *recognition* of the gift or the giver on the part of the receiver is equal to compensation (which, of course, nullifies the gift as well).[95] The character of gratuitousness is itself the problematic—it does not

---

[90] Here I mean matter as body or material, not matter as issue or problem.

[91] Derrida, *Given Time*, 11.

[92] This is not to say that each component must be recognized by the others; rather, the gift needs to have each of these three parts to be considered any kind of transfer at all.

[93] Derrida, *Given Time*, 11.

[94] Ibid., 12.

[95] Ibid., 12, 13, 14, 16, 23.

on its own make the gift the impossible, but joining it to the structure and matter of the gift does.

The third constitutive element of the gift—its matter—has to do with its necessary dependence on systems of economy and value. While the gift must be gratuitous, the gift itself must have some value in order to qualify as a gift. What gift could be a gift if it were in no sense valuable, at least to some degree? Further, a gift's value is generally determined by an economy, whether it is of simple economy or of symbolic value. This is what Derrida means when he says, "Now the gift, *if there is any*, would no doubt be related to economy. One cannot treat the gift . . . without treating this relation to economy, even to the money economy."[96] The point for Derrida is that the gift is inseparable from value and economy, on the one hand, but that, on the other, it *must* be in a way separated from value and economy. The circle of economic exchange is assumed by the gift, but it must remain foreign to the gift. In Derrida's words, "If the figure of the circle is essential to economics, the gift must remain *aneconomic*. Not that it remains foreign to the circle, but it must *keep* a relation of foreignness to the circle."[97] If the gift touches economy, then it is no longer a gift, but if it is completely separated from economy, then likewise it is no longer a gift. Again, this on its own does not preclude the possibility of the gift, but when it is taken with the other two constitutive elements, the gift remains the impossible.

While Derrida goes to lengths to explain why the gift is the impossible, he nevertheless does not completely rule out the gift's reality. Derrida circumvents the inherent impossibility of the gift by arguing that the gift, if there is any, takes place only on the condition of forgetting.[98] For Derrida, if the gift is recognized as what it is, it vanishes. Recognizing the gift as what it is would require seeing the structure, character, and matter all at the same time—and that is exactly what is impossible about the gift. The very constitution of the gift makes it the impossible, so recognition or remembrance of the gift jars it out of reality and hides it again in impossibility. Derrida does not argue that the gift is an impossible phenomenon; instead, he argues that it cannot present itself *as* a phenomenon, because as a phenomenon it is the impossible. In Derrida's words, "The gift *itself*—we dare not say the gift in *itself*—will

---

[96] Derrida, *Given Time*, 7. Emphasis in original.
[97] Ibid. Emphases in original.
[98] Derrida, *Given Time*, 16–18.

never be confused with the presence of its phenomenon."[99] Therefore, for the gift to take place, it relies completely on the condition of forgetting—both the forgetting of the giver and of the receiver.

In their own ways, Heidegger, Mauss, and Derrida each provides an essential part of the philosophical backdrop against which Chauvet plays out his theology. Chauvet, of course, also draws from explicitly theological sources, but these will be attended to in greater detail in chapter 3. At this point, having situated Chauvet in the philosophical context in which his work unfolds, this discussion now turns to situating Luther in the interpretive context relevant to this discussion, that is, to summarizing the major interpretations of Luther that will frame the second chapter's study.

Background: Strains of Luther Interpretation

The work of Martin Luther has shaped the trajectories of Western Christian theology in more ways than can be concisely summarized here. While his thought has inspired the theologies of a number of traditions in various ways, this discussion focuses on one emerging vein of interpretation of Luther and adopts it as a kind of hermeneutic through which to read his work on the connection between sacraments and ethics. The New Finnish Interpretation of Luther, with its emphasis on justification as unification with Christ, will provide in chapters 2 and 4 something of a new way of engaging a Roman Catholic conversation partner in Chauvet. A conversation across the Tiber on the connection between sacraments and ethics could easily rehearse the familiar ground of forensic justification, faith formed by charity, real presence, transubstantiation, and any number of other themes that tend to crop up in Lutheran–Roman Catholic discourse. While such themes are certainly important, adopting the hermeneutic of the Finnish School will afford this project a new light under which to address the connection of sacraments and ethics. Therefore, some explanation of the origins and themes of the Finnish School is necessary to situate the discussion.

With that said, if the goal of this book is a conversation across the Tiber, it would behoove us to attend to those who have been wary of such endeavors, such as interpreters of Luther who would be unwilling to surrender the language of forensic justification or divine imputation.

[99] Ibid., 29.

Consequently, the second half of this section will appropriate the work of one such scholar in an effort to summarize the essential points of this position. In a word, if this discussion adopts the hermeneutic of the Finnish School, what insights of Luther's must it take particular care to preserve in order to remain faithful to his theology and heritage?

The New Finnish Interpretation of Luther (The Finnish School)

The New Finnish Interpretation of Luther (hereafter the "Finnish School") has its origins in the thought of Tuomo Mannermaa, an emeritus professor of church history at the University of Helsinki. Mannermaa, drawing initial inspiration from Regin Prenter and Georg Kretschmar,[100] has argued that within Luther's thought there is a conception of justification and sanctification that is analogous to the Eastern Orthodox concept of *theosis*. A good deal of the work of the Finnish School has in fact been done in the context of conversations between Finnish Lutherans and Russian Orthodox.[101] Mannermaa's main point is that when Luther speaks about justification, he often does so by claiming Christ becomes really—even substantially—present in the believer by faith.[102] In contradistinction to the more traditional interpretation of Luther as maintaining a more "forensic" view of justification (which will be outlined below), Mannermaa's reading of Luther emphasizes in large part the participation of the believer in the very person of Christ.

In order to maintain this reading of Luther as valid, Mannermaa takes pains to distinguish the thought of Luther himself from the

---

[100] Tuomo Mannermaa, *Christ Present in Faith: Luther's View of Justification* (Minneapolis: Fortress, 2005), 7. Mannermaa cites a specific work by Regin Prenter (*Theologie und Gottesdienst: Gesammelte Aufsätze* [Arhus: Aros, 1977], 289, n. 10) and explains that he drew support and encouragement for his work both from an article by Kretschmar and extensive subsequent conversations with him (specifically, Georg Kretschmar, "Kreutz und Auferstehung in der Sicht von Athanasios und Luther," in *Der Auferstandene Christus und das Heil der Welt. Das Kirchberger Gespräch über die Bedeutung der Auferstehung für das Heil der Welt zwischen Vertretern der Evangelischen Kirche in Deutschland und Ruschischen Orthodoxen Kirche*, ed. Kirchliches Ausenamt der EKD, Studienheft 7 [Witten: Luther Verlag, 1972], 40–82.).

[101] Tuomo Mannermaa, "Why Is Luther so Fascinating? Modern Finnish Luther Research," in *Union with Christ: The New Finnish Interpretation of Luther*, ed. Carl E. Braaten and Robert W. Jenson (Grand Rapids, MI: Wm. B. Eerdmans, 1998), 1.

[102] Mannermaa, *Christ Present in Faith*, 18.

thought and formulae of Lutherans that came after him. Mannermaa acknowledges the fact that the Lutheran confessional statements are basically not in accord with his reading of Luther's thought, but he nevertheless maintains that a fresh interpretation of Luther on justification is a legitimate and worthwhile exercise.[103] One of the main reasons for his boldness in doing so is that the language of the Lutheran confessional documents, most notably the *Formula of Concord*, points back to Luther himself. When the *Formula* explains justification, it finishes the discussion with a reference to Luther's *Lectures on Galations*, which is far and away the text Mannermaa cites most often and most substantively. Mannermaa also points out that the *Formula* not only cites Luther but also gives Luther's theology sway in this regard over its own articulations.[104] In this way, Mannermaa maintains, the *Formula* leaves open the question of what exactly Luther taught about justification, which gives his interpretation—based as it is on Luther's *Lectures on Galatians*—at least some weight for Lutherans beyond Luther himself.

Mannermaa's point of departure for his project is Luther's concept of Christ as *maxima persona*, "the greatest person," or a kind of corporate person in whom the entire human race is united.[105] The importance of this concept goes beyond thinking of Christ just as the "new Adam"; when speaking of sin and salvation, conceiving of Christ as the *maxima persona* carries with it the conception of Christ as the *maximus peccator* (greatest sinner) and even *solus peccator* (only sinner).[106] If the entirety of our fallen humanity is united in the person of Christ, then the person of Christ contains the sin of the whole world. Or, more correctly, the thought process is *vice versa*: since we know the sins of the whole world have been heaped upon Christ, we can speak of fallen humanity wholly contained in—that is, united in—Christ.[107] The sinfulness of humankind is located entirely in Christ, and sin and death are then obliterated by Christ's life, death, and resurrection.

At this point, the seed of Mannermaa's thesis becomes apparent: if Christ is *solus peccator*, that is, if Christ's humanity implies the real participation by the entirety of fallen human nature in the person of Christ, then salvation ought to be conceived of in a similar way, namely, that

[103] Ibid., 5.
[104] Ibid.
[105] Ibid., 15.
[106] Ibid.
[107] Luther, *Lectures on Galatians*, quoted in Mannermaa, *Christ Present in Faith*, 15.

Christ's redemption of humanity implies the real participation by every redeemed human in the person of Christ. Put another way, justifying faith is a real participation in the person of Christ.[108]

Such participation is the linchpin of Mannermaa's project and the central theme of the Finnish School—Christian participation in Christ's person (that is, even in God's very essence in Christ) is not solely a moment of divine-human contact; it is also a unification of lives: the human life with Christ's life. To explain this, Mannermaa lifts up Luther's explanations of Christ as both the favor (*favor*) of God and also the gift (*donum*) of God. Put simply, God's favor is given through Christ to the human person in the form of forgiveness. As the human is bound through faith to Christ, in whom all sin has been gathered together and defeated, the human is thereby purged of sin.[109] This purgation is not, however, purely a once-for-all or momentary action by God; this forgiveness—this favor—is accompanied by God's gift (*donum*) of Christ, which persists beyond the moment of forgiveness. Christ as God's gift means that the whole Christ—divine nature and all—is given to the Christian. The Christian then becomes a participant in Christ—again, divine nature and all—as Christ now dwells in the human through faith.[110]

One would need to be careful about reading into this distinction between Christ as *favor* and Christ as *bonum* the distinction between justification and sanctification. While the distinction is roughly analogous, Mannermaa takes pains to maintain that the separation of the concepts of justification and sanctification is in fact alien to Luther.[111] For Luther, the unification of the Christian with Christ constitutes a single process, which can be spoken of by distinct terms. The distinction in Luther between justification and sanctification can be roughly conceived of as the distinction between faith and works (or between faith and Christian holiness).[112] As such, this distinction is not one of order in a process, as if faith is step 1 and works are step 2. Instead, the relationship between faith and works for Luther, in the reading of the Finnish School, is one of form and matter. Again, the form of faith is Christ, but faith is the form of works.[113] In this way, Christ becomes incarnate in the works of Christians, but such works are not separate

---

[108] Mannermaa, *Christ Present in Faith*, 17.

[109] Luther, *Lectures on Galatians*, quoted in Mannermaa, *Christ Present in Faith*, 18.

[110] Mannermaa, *Christ Present in Faith*, 19–22.

[111] Ibid., 49.

[112] Ibid., 46, 49.

[113] Ibid., 46.

from the event of justification, since all these concepts are connected directly to the presence of Christ in the believer through faith. This is the basis of the Finnish School and also its culmination—Christ is really present in the Christian through faith, which implies that Christian life is a real participation in the very divine life of Christ.

The Luther of Justification by Divine Imputation

Divinely imputed justification (sometimes referred to as "forensic" justification—a term I will tend to avoid, for reasons to be fleshed out below) is one of the mainstays of Luther interpretation. Lutherans and non-Lutherans alike associate this concept with the Reformer and the ecclesial tradition he inspired,[114] and it is inextricable from any careful reflection on Luther's ideas of grace and salvation. To set the background for this concept in Luther, I use here mainly the thought of Gerhard O. Forde, not because he is the only theologian to carefully consider this area of Luther's thought, but because a representative example will better serve to set up this idea than would attempting to distill into a few pages the entirety of scholarship on the subject.[115] The thought of Forde provides a worthwhile counterpoint to the Finnish School; while the Finnish School has been forged in and further developed with an eye to ecumenical conversation (specifically with the Orthodox), Forde's writings embody a kind of hesitancy—or in some cases outright suspicion—toward ecumenical dialogues, because of a perceived lack of theological rigor with which he thought they often treat the doctrine of justification.[116]

---

[114] See, for example, Stephen J. Duffy, *The Dynamics of Grace: Perspectives in Theological Anthropology* (Collegeville, MN: Liturgical Press, 1993), 173–220. For a survey of the ways justification has been discussed between Lutherans and Roman Catholics, see Pieter de Witte, *Doctrine, Dynamic and Difference: To the Heart of the Lutheran–Roman Catholic Differentiated Consensus on Justification* (New York: Continuum, 2012).

[115] For some other perspectives, see B. A. Gerrish, *Grace and Reason: A Study in the Theology of Luther* (Eugene, OR: Wipf & Stock, 2005); Heinrich Bornkamm, *Luther's World of Thought*, trans. Martin H. Bertram (St. Louis, MO: Concordia, 2001); or Gerhard Ebeling, *Luther: An Introduction to His Thought*, trans. R. A. Wilson (Minneapolis, MN: Fortress, 2007).

[116] Perhaps the clearest example of this suspicion was Forde's open critique of the 1999 Joint Declaration on the Doctrine of Justification. See Gerhard Forde, "The Critical Response of German Theological Professors to the Joint Declaration on Justification," *dialog* 38 (1999): 71–72; and Forde, et. al., "A Call for Discussion of the 'Joint Declaration on the Doctrine of Justification,'" *dialog* 36 (1997): 224–29.

Forde's work and thinking in this vein made him a key figure in what has been called "radical Lutheranism," that is, a movement within Lutheranism whose chief aim has been to keep the Lutheran confessional doctrine of justification at the forefront of Lutheran theological inquiry.[117] While this movement is not necessarily the most influential or representative take on Luther's thought and the Lutheran confessions, its ardent focus on the doctrine of justification makes it invaluable for this project; whatever else may be said of Forde and radical Lutheranism, they have been quite careful about parsing out Lutheran thought on justification and grace.

As Forde reads Luther, two distinct paradigms frame the doctrine of justification—paradigms he maintains ought to be complementary. (He does not, however, think they should both be paradigms of justification *per se*; one he associates with justification, and the other he associates with discovery of one's guilt.) The first paradigm is the legal metaphor, wherein we guilty sinners are forgiven by God and held justified. The second is the metaphor of dying to sin and rising to new life.[118] Within Lutheranism, both of these metaphors attempt to make sense of justification by divine imputation. (This is the term Forde prefers to the label "forensic" justification, though for all practical purposes the terms seem to connote the same thing.) Justification by divine imputation implies that justification is an action only of God, given to humans regardless of human action or lack thereof. Luther's concept of *sola fide* is closely tied to justification by divine imputation, and Forde depends heavily on it to explain his views on both the legal metaphor of justification and the death/life metaphor.

Forde's work with the legal metaphor for justification generally appears in the form of a critique of the metaphor, but before we move to using his critiques to clarify the metaphor, what exactly is the legal metaphor for justification? At its base, Forde maintains, the legal metaphor is exactly what it sounds like: a metaphor based on the law.[119] That the legal metaphor works when speaking about the fall or sin hardly needs explanation (God ordered things a certain way, and we humans are guilty of marring that), but the temptation to carry that metaphor

---

[117] Joseph A. Burgess and Marc Kolden, "Introduction: Gerhard O. Forde and the Doctrine of Justification," in *By Faith Alone: Essays on Justification in Honor of Gerhard O. Forde* (Grand Rapids, MI: Wm. B. Eerdmans, 2004), 7.

[118] Gerhard O. Forde, *Justification by Faith: A Matter of Death and Life* (Philadelphia: Fortress, 1982), 3–4, 8–9.

[119] Ibid., 13.

through as the primary way to speak about justification can be problematic. In fact, Forde argues that this is the major temptation against which Luther argues with the emphasis on *sola fide*.[120] In the legal metaphor, if we humans are guilty before God, then justification ought to imply some process by which we humans change from guilty to guiltless. That justification can be conceived of as a *process* or a *movement* is the heart of the legal metaphor of justification, Forde maintains.[121] He locates the "finest form" of this conception in Thomas Aquinas's *Summa Theologiae*:

> Thomas Aquinas . . . defines justification as a movement from a *terminus a quo* to a *terminus ad quem* (a movement from a starting point to a finishing point) involving several steps: a) the infusion of grace (grace *does* come first); b) the movement of the free will toward God in faith; c) the movement of the free will in recoil from sin; and d) remission of guilt.[122]

Forde does acknowledge that this process of justification in Thomas is not a temporal step-by-step progression, but he nevertheless maintains that in the very structure of conceiving of justification as a process, "the way is open, no doubt, for precisely those distortions which *did* occur in the middle ages."[123] This is the tendency to which Luther was so opposed in adhering to justification by divine imputation and *sola fide*. Justification as a process can lend itself easily to questions of whether one step or another is "fulfilled," because certainly the human ought to be *doing* something in this movement—or at least we humans ought to *see something happening*. This, for Forde, is where Lutheran views of justification differ from a great portion of Roman Catholic conceptions; in Forde's view of Luther's thought, there is no necessary outward change that accompanies justification. Moral progress might be a result of justification, but it has nothing intrinsically to do with justification itself.

---

[120] Ibid., 23–26.

[121] Ibid., 25.

[122] Ibid. Also, from Thomas Aquinas: "There are four things which are accounted to be necessary for the justification of the ungodly, namely, the infusion of grace, the movement of the free will toward God by faith, the movement of the free will toward sin, and the remission of sins" (*Summa Theologiae* I–II, q. 113, art. 6; Respondeo dicetum quod quatuor enumerantur quae requiruntur ad iustificationem impii, scilicet gratiae infusio; motus liberi arbitrii in Deum per fidem; et motus liberi arbitrii in peccatum; et remissio culpae).

[123] Forde, *Justification by Faith*, 25.

Forde's point is that the unconditional nature of justification implied by Luther's *sola fide* militates against the legal metaphor, given as the metaphor is to being thought of as a process, or necessarily including some kind of change or progress. The nagging thought of "surely we humans ought to do *something* for justification" is ever present in the legal metaphor, and any tendency toward that way of thinking, for Forde, misses the point Luther was making with justification by faith alone or justification by divine imputation.[124] As Forde sees the situation, it can be rather easy for Lutherans to qualify away Luther's *sola fide*. "Adverbial" language about faith and justification creeps in and attempts to make *sola fide* work with the legal metaphor: "*really* believing," "*sincere, heartfelt* trust," "*living, active* faith," "*deep* repentance," or other such ideas.[125] For Luther, these may be all well and good, but they are not criteria for justification. The *sola fide* of justification—that it is through faith and by divine imputation—admits of no prerequisites, and the legal metaphor is full of tendencies toward exactly that.

The metaphor that, for Forde, works immeasurably better (that is not to say it works perfectly) in speaking about justification by divine imputation is the metaphor of Romans 6: that of death and new life. Instead of moving through a process of becoming guiltless when we humans were once guilty, Luther's take on justification is that humans become alive when they were once *dead*. This is why Forde maintains that the legal metaphor and the death-life metaphor are complementary; the legal metaphor works so far as the law is concerned, but when grace enters the mix, death and life is the proper metaphor. In Forde's words:

> The order of the legal metaphor is always life-death. You can do the law only as long as you are alive; you have to earn your points while you can. For the legal metaphor is a matter, as we say, of "life and death." When you die it's too late. If you die you shall not live. The law grants possibility up to death; after death, no more possibility.[126]

The point Forde makes here is that we humans, by sin, are all in the "after death" part of the equation. The law defines the boundaries, and we humans have crossed them into sin and death. Consequently, justification cannot be just a removal of guilt while humans are dead to sin; such a move attempts to take the legal metaphor beyond its own limits;

124 Ibid., 9.
125 Ibid., 10.
126 Ibid., 13.

that is, if humans are already dead in sin, no change or process can (within the legal metaphor) "fix" the deadness. Humans are *dead* in sin; what is needed is *life*, not law. Such life is precisely what Luther sees in justification by divine imputation, or the *sola fide* of justification: it is a resurrection of the human into *new* life, not a continuation of the old "life" that was sin and death. What is, under the legal metaphor, a "repair" of a continuously existing human subject is, under the death/life metaphor, the resurrection of the dead human to new life in Christ.[127] In a word, the complementarity of the legal metaphor with the death-life metaphor is, in Forde's interpretation of Luther, the "complementarity" of the law and the gospel. The law kills, and the gospel makes alive. Humans are dead in sin, condemned by the law, but in justification they are raised to new life in Christ.

One ought to ask the question at this point, what exactly does the death-life metaphor evoke from Luther that solves or avoids the problems with which the legal metaphor collides? Should humans not still see some "progress" associated with being resurrected out of death and sin? Isn't there still a "process" or "movement" from death into life? Forde addresses these questions not by answering them directly but by pointing out that within the death-life metaphor through which Luther views justification—again, that Forde sees as the only appropriate one—such questions are the incorrect ones to ask; they border on category mistakes. Movement or progress assumes a *terminus a quo* and *terminus ad quem*, and death and life are inappropriate stand-ins for these terms; humans do not move *from* death *into* life. Humans are resurrected: they are dead in sin, and God raises them. There is no discernable process (humanly speaking); the whole affair is the action of God, for which humans do not have criteria or readily readable markers.

In this vein, one might also ask the question of whether faith itself is not some kind of process or—even more problematically—some kind of human action. In Luther, divine imputation and *sola fide* go together, so how is the imputation not consequent upon a *sola fide* action? Such a question is hardly new, but again Forde maintains that, in Luther, this is a category mistake. Faith, Forde maintains, is for Luther "not an active verb. . . . It is a state-of-being verb."[128] Faith is not an assent of the intellect, nor is it a conviction of the will, nor is it even a conscious trust, insofar as such trust requires human action. Faith can be conceived of

---

[127] Ibid., 17.
[128] Ibid., 22.

as "trust," but it is more of a passive trust, bordering on simple recognition of the state of reality (not unlike someone may be said to "trust" in gravity). In Forde's words, "Faith is the state of being grasped by the unconditional claim and promise of the God who calls into being that which is from that which is not. Faith means now having to deal with life on those terms. It is a death and a resurrection."[129]

By faith humans recognize a new situation, one different from the old situation of sin and death. (Or, more correctly, they recognize the old situation of sin and death as the old situation of sin and death, and this recognition itself *is* a new situation.) This is the way in which Luther's concept of justification by divine imputation requires *sola fide* and *vice versa*. God declares the human justified, and in doing so reveals the human's sin for what it is. Justification by divine imputation includes not simply imputed justice but also the revelation by faith (*sola fide*) of human sinfulness: "By declaring us righteous unilaterally, unconditionally for Christ's sake, [God] at the same time unmasks sin and unfaith."[130]

The question may remain, however, that if justification by divine imputation and by faith alone requires a departure from the legal metaphor, what can be said of sanctification in Luther? I bring this up not because sanctification is the primary focus here, but because the temptation to use the legal metaphor—the metaphor of process and progress—has a tendency to return in full force after being expunged from the theology of justification. If human life can be characterized by a daily dying to sin and rising again in Christ,[131] then surely we may be able to speak of the whole set of those human experiences as an overall "process" of sanctification. Luther's answer to this (so Forde maintains) is only a certain kind of yes:

> The "progress" of the Christian . . . is the progress of one who has constantly to get used to the fact that we are justified totally by faith, constantly has somehow to "recover," so to speak, from that death blow to pride and presumption—or better, is constantly being raised from the tomb of all pious ambition to something quite new. The believer has to

---

[129] Ibid.

[130] Ibid., 31.

[131] This is something Luther wanted all Christians to connect with the sacraments (particularly baptism), as he includes the idea in his *Small Catechism* (Martin Luther, *The Small Catechism*, in *The Book of Concord*, ed. Timothy J. Wengert and Robert Kolb, trans. Charles Arand, et al., [Minneapolis, Fortress, 2000], 360).

be renewed daily in that. The Old Being is to be drowned daily in repentance and raised in faith. The progress in the Christian life is not our movement toward the goal; it is the movement of the goal in upon us.[132]

For Forde, what is ultimately at stake in emphasizing the death and life metaphor for justification (and sanctification) is the heart of Luther's theology itself. To his reading, losing sight of justification as divinely imputed—as he might say the Finnish School does, in its formula of justification as unification with Christ—endangers the core insights of Reformation theology in general, and Lutheran theology in particular. That said, this book proceeds with the conviction that these two Lutheran models for conceiving of justification can stand together. Further, as we will see in chapter 2, this project adopts the Finnish School as a hermeneutic, not to circumvent Luther's insights regarding justification, but to cast new light on them, especially as they play out at the intersection between sacraments and ethics.

Conclusion

This chapter has provided four areas of background information on which to base the following chapter discussions and within which those discussions fit. To begin, the chapter summarized the development of the Liturgical Movement in the United States, highlighting some of its main proponents and tracing it through the Second Vatican Council. Then, the chapter briefly focused on three theologians whose work represents at least partially the current avenues of inquiry in the field of liturgy and ethics. Next, the chapter traced the philosophical influences that bear upon Chauvet's theology, especially as it will be engaged in this project. Finally, the chapter closed by reviewing two strains of Luther interpretation, the Finnish school that will provide the hermeneutical approach of this project's engagement with Luther, and Forde's radical Lutheranism that provides a caution against being swept away from Luther's core insights. Having done all this, the book is situated in an ideal spot to proceed, which it does by engaging Luther and the way he views the connection of sacraments and ethics.

---

[132] Forde, *Justification by Faith*, 31.

Chapter 2

Sacraments and Ethics
in Martin Luther

Introduction

At first glance, the project of mining the thought of Martin Luther in order to discover a connection between sacraments and ethics may seem like a questionable pursuit. Dominated as Luther's thought is by the concept of justification by faith alone apart from works, any attempt to see in Luther a connection between God's justifying (and, as we will see, sanctifying) action in the sacraments, on the one hand, and Christians' ethical lives, on the other, runs the risk of minimizing Luther's stark distinction between justification and works. In order to remain faithful to Luther's central insight, this discussion employs one of Luther's central texts on justification by faith—his commentary on Galatians—and argues ultimately that, for Luther, sacraments and ethics are connected by the unification of the Christian with Christ, which is the operation of sacramental grace.

In order to reach this conclusion, this chapter begins by outlining Luther's sacramental theology. For Luther, the sacraments provide a place and practice where salvation history unfolds in the lives of Christians. More specifically, God's action within the sacraments brings salvation to those who participate, which provides the basis for Luther's subsequent thought on how Christians live, having experienced God's

41

saving grace.[1] Exactly how God's action in the sacraments does this is the subject of the first section of this chapter, which proceeds according to a trifold conceptual framework: First, the discussion highlights God's giving, that is, God's saving action on behalf of humans, and how that grounds Luther's sacramental theology. Second, the discussion turns to the concept of God's promises—namely, the promises of forgiveness of sins and life everlasting—as the guarantees of salvation that are accessible by faith alone. Third, the discussion turns to the issue of God's presence, which will provide a bridge to speaking of the unification of Christians with Christ. The section then finishes by examining the "why" of the sacraments in Luther, namely, that in Luther's thought the sacraments effect both justification and love.

Having brought out the high points of Luther's sacramental theology, the chapter turns in its second section to what exactly justification is. The Finnish School provides the cornerstone for this discussion, that justification is a unification of the believer with Christ. While the Finnish School has gained a considerable following recently (particularly in North America), this discussion employs it more as a hermeneutic than as an interpretation in itself. The Finnish School provides something in discussing sacraments and ethics that the more traditional Lutheran view of justification strictly by divine imputation cannot: the valuing of ethics as intrinsic to the identity of a Christian rather than acts merely added on to the justified Christian as a kind of exercise of gratitude to God.[2] To explain more fully what this unification with Christ entails, the discussion focuses on the concepts of Christian righteousness and active righteousness in Luther. Further, these concepts help throw into sharper relief what unification with Christ does *not* entail. (That is, unification with Christ is effected by faith, and this passively; Luther takes care to stay away from the idea that any works, even works of love,

---

[1] This is not to say that for Luther the sacraments are the exclusive place where the salvation of humans is accomplished. The cross and resurrection are where God once and for all saved humankind in Luther's thought, but in the sacraments that salvation wrought definitively by Christ becomes a part of the concrete existence of Christians.

[2] This ought not to suggest that for the Finnish School ethics defines the Christian, as if ethical action could be a litmus test for "real" Christian identity. Such an idea is foreign to Luther. Rather, this line of thought (as we will develop below) simply suggests that union with Christ very much includes ethics as part of one's identity, because how could it not?

can either assist with or perfect this unification.) Springing from this is a conception of ethics as Christ-in-us, which the remainder of the chapter fleshes out.

The model of ethics as Christ-in-us finds expression in two main areas of Luther's thought: his view of the Christian as *simul iustus et peccator* and his view of sanctification. The Christian as *simul iustus et peccator* encapsulates Luther's view of what Christian life after justification looks like. The Christian, now unified with Christ, nevertheless remains a sinner, at least to the extent that the propensity to sin (a sin in itself for Luther) never fully leaves the human, even when the human is held justified by God in Christ. This is why, Luther explains, humans do not magically transform into pillars of moral living immediately upon justification; they have been unified with Christ, but the old human still lives within them. Furthermore, the second area of expression of ethics as Christ-in-us—sanctification—is not simply the process of becoming increasingly proficient in denying the old human and acting as Christ. For Luther, unification with Christ includes sanctification in itself, because how can one become *more* sanctified than when one is unified with Christ?[3] Sanctification takes place in Christian life moving forward from justification, but sanctification is not the same as moral development or growth. This is not a conflation of justification and sanctification; there still exists a distinction between these two in Luther, but sanctification in his thought is nevertheless not about a process of moral progress.

Luther on the Sacraments

For Luther, the sacraments are rituals in which the Christian comes into intimate contact with God and God's action. In the sacraments (which, for the purposes of this section, are baptism and the Eucharist),[4] God's promises of forgiveness of sins and life everlasting become present

---

[3] Forde, *Justification by Faith*, 50–51.

[4] Luther himself largely emphasized baptism and Eucharist as the two central and only sacraments, but he did for a time consider penance a sacrament, See Martin Luther, "The Babylonian Captivity of the Church," in *Word and Sacrament II*, vol. 36 of *Luther's Works*, ed. Abdel Ross Wentz and Helmut T. Lehmann (Philadelphia, PA: Fortress Press, 1959), 81–91. Moving forward, all citations of Martin Luther are from *Luther's Works* (abbreviated *LW*), American ed., 55 vols, ed. Jaroslav Pelikan and Helmut T. Lehmann (Philadelphia: Muhlenberg and Fortress, and Saint Louis: Concordia, 1955–1986).

in and as Christ's sacramental presence, justifying the Christian and inspiring subsequent Christian life. In order to map out Luther's sacramental theology, this section proceeds in three steps: God's giving, God's promises, and God's presence. This triad of God's giving, promises, and presence (while not specifically a construction Luther himself uses) provides an apt conceptual framework within which this discussion locates Luther's thought on the sacraments. First, the section begins with a discussion of what Luther sees as God's action in the sacraments, namely, God's action of giving. For Luther, the bulk of sacramental theology concerns God's saving action on behalf of humans, given in God's gifts of promise and presence. Understanding first *that* the sacraments are God's actions of giving paves the way for this discussion's second topic, the specific gift of God's promises of forgiveness of sins and life everlasting. What Luther means by these and how he believes Christians receive them (i.e., by faith) provides the basis for the third part of this section: discussing the gift of God's sacramental presence in Christ. Having unpacked Luther's thinking on God's giving, promises, and presence, this section ends by briefly turning to the "why" of sacraments for Luther. The purposes of the sacraments (which for Luther are, first, justification and, second, love) provide a bridge to the second part of this chapter: a model of Luther's thinking concerning ethics as Christ-in-us.

God's Action in Giving, Presence, and Promise

Rather than beginning with a study of exactly *what* Luther might mean by the concept of a sacrament, the point of departure in this section is what *happens* for Luther in the context of the sacraments. Questions of definition, of what Luther means when he uses the words "liturgy," "sacrament," "worship," "Mass," or other similar terms, are not without worth; however, in the context of the present discussion (namely, exploring the connection between sacraments and ethics) it is the *action*—more specifically the *giving*—that takes place in the sacraments that is most important. To ask first what a sacrament is and then subsequently move to the question of what happens therein shifts the framework of the discussion away from Luther's fundamental starting point in his sacramental theology: God's action of giving in Christ's promise and presence. What a sacrament is for Luther is tied immediately to what God *does* therein.[5] Put another way, the foundation of

---

[5] It is significant that in Luther's most systematic treatise on the sacraments, "The Babylonian Captivity of the Church," he calls "the most wicked abuse of [the

Luther's sacramental theology is grace, which in the context of liturgy and the sacraments manifests as Christ's active gift of presence and promise.

In naming the triad of Christ's gift, presence, and promise I do not mean to separate those three; I mean simply to use them as interconnected ways of speaking about Luther's concept of what happens in sacraments and liturgy. In Luther's thought, these concepts are found together, as parts of a whole (i.e., God's gift of presence or God's gift of the promise, neither concept of which can do without the other). For example, first, Luther is concerned nearly wherever he speaks of sacraments to emphasize that they are actions of divine giving, not good works done by humans. Luther argues this most clearly in *The Babylonian Captivity of the Church* (1520), where he calls "by far the most wicked abuse of all" the eucharistic practice that leads to the view "that the mass is a good work and a sacrifice."[6] Luther's sacramental theology is, of course, not exhausted by eucharistic theology, but the Eucharist does provide a telling example of how Luther views the way sacraments operate.[7] As such, what follows in this section concentrates mostly on

---

Eucharist]" the idea that the Eucharist is a human work of sacrifice rather than a divine gift (*LW* 36:35). In the same treatise regarding baptism, Luther states, "the *first* thing to be considered about baptism is the divine promise," the action of God on humans' behalf, as opposed to "works, vows, religious orders, and whatever else man has introduced" (ibid., 58–59). Even concerning penance—which Luther first considered a sacrament and then later did not—Luther states that "this sacrament, like the other two, consists in the word of divine promise and our faith" (ibid., 81–82), both components of which (divine promise and our faith) are ultimately for him actions of God.

  [6] Luther, "The Babylonian Captivity," *LW* 36:35.

  [7] It is true that infant baptism also embodies Luther's view of how sacraments work—i.e., they bring justification and salvation to particular humans (Luther, "The Babylonian Captivity," *LW* 36:58–59). It is also important to note, however, that when Luther speaks of baptism, he is careful to point out that "it is not baptism that justifies or benefits anyone, but it is the faith in that word of promise to which baptism is added" (ibid., 66). This, coupled with Luther's explanation of the faith of infants as reliant upon those who bring them for baptism (ibid., 73), would slightly confuse the issue for the purposes of the present discussion because it juxtaposes the particularity of individual human reception of God's saving action with a participation in a kind of communal faith. Such juxtaposition might evoke some of Chauvet's conceptions of communality, but I am not sure the two concepts would harmonize well. As such, and given that the current discussion can accomplish its goal without relying heavily on Luther's conception of specifically infant baptism, the book moves forward with the bulk of its attention paid to the Eucharist.

the Eucharist/the Mass. For Luther, the active party in sacraments generally, and the Eucharist in particular, is God in Christ. This is why he is so opposed to the Mass as a sacrifice; in the Eucharist, we humans receive. We do not offer. In Luther's view, to speak of the Mass as a sacrifice implies that in the Eucharist we humans offer something to God, which places the agency in humans rather than on the part of God in Christ.[8] A sacrifice is something given, while a testament—the term Luther lifts up from the words of institution as the primary description of the Eucharist—is for him something received.[9] To speak of Christians sacrificing to God, which for Luther is ultimately where viewing the Mass as sacrifice leads, is, in Luther's view, absurd. In the Eucharist, God gives, and we humans receive—never *vice versa*.

To be fair, Luther does allow that the prayers the church offers together in the context of the liturgy may be viewed as good works (and even Sacrifices), but he takes care to distinguish them from the sacrament/Mass itself.[10] In his words, "These [prayers] are not the mass, but works of the mass—if prayers of the heart and lips may be called works—for they flow from the faith that is kindled or increased in the sacrament."[11] Between the sacrament of the Mass and works of the Mass Luther sees a clear distinction—not of participation, but of the subject of that participation.[12] In the sacrament of the Mass, the active subject is God in Christ, who creates and animates faith in passive human participants, while in the works of the Mass those who were passive human participants begin to live out the faith awakened in them through prayers they offer for themselves and others. That these actions can occur simultaneously in the liturgy is of no consequence for Luther; reception

[8] A good deal of work has been done recently on the concept of sacrifice, specifically to interpret it as an action of God in the context of the Eucharist. See, for example, Edward Kilmartin, *The Eucharist in the West* (Collegeville, MN: Liturgical Press, 2004), or Robert J. Daly, *Sacrifice Unveiled: The True Meaning of Christian Sacrifice* (New York: T&T Clark, 2009). Luther's vehemence on this subject, however, suggests that in his context such interpretations of sacrifice were at best secondary to a more common interpretation of sacrifice in which the Sacrament of the Altar was a meritorious work performed upon human initiative.

[9] Luther, "Babylonian Captivity," *LW* 36:37.

[10] Ibid., 50.

[11] Ibid.

[12] I recognize that the term "subject" here is anachronistic. I do not mean to insert a post-Enlightenment concept of the subject into Luther; I simply mean to use it to help illuminate difference of actions Luther sees in Christian liturgy.

of the sacrament is passive reception, while any Christian action remains consequent upon that reception in faith.[13]

If we grant with Luther that in the sacrament of the Mass God acts and gives rather than we humans, we can legitimately ask, what does God give? Luther's answer is simple: God gives to humans salvation and does so in two modes. First, God gives God's presence in Christ (bearing witness to God's promises of salvation), and, second, God gives God's promise in Christ (making God's presence active and salvific). These two concepts—God's presence and God's promise—are distinct but not separate in Luther's thought; God's presence embodies God's promise, and God's promise vivifies God's presence.

For Luther, the presence of Christ in the sacraments bears witness to God's promises of salvation in that this is the reason we humans take part in the sacraments (particularly the Eucharist) at all. In Luther's words, "[Christ] commands that you take his body and blood. Why? For what reason? Because the body is given for you and the blood is poured out for you."[14] God's gift of God's self in Christ occurred definitively in the incarnation and on the cross, but that gift comes to each individual human in the human's participation in the sacraments: "When I say: 'This is the body, which is given for you, this is the blood, which is poured out for you for the forgiveness of sins,' I am there commemorating [Christ]; I proclaim and announce his death. Only it is not done publicly in the congregation but is directed at you alone."[15] Christ's presence in the sacraments is *for* us humans, and receiving that presence is salvific in Luther's view simply because that is how God has chosen to make salvation available.[16] Put another way, this is what God has promised.

This is why God's promise makes the presence of Christ active and salvific. God's promise of salvation is the gift that humans receive by God's presence. It is the assurance of salvation on which the entirety of Christian hope rests. In Luther's words, "Unless we firmly hold that the mass is the promise or testament of Christ, as the words clearly say, we shall lose the whole gospel and all its comfort."[17] For Luther, everything

---

[13] Luther, "Babylonian Captivity," *LW* 36:50–51.

[14] Luther, "The Sacrament of the Body and Blood of Christ—Against the Fanatics," *LW* 36:348.

[15] Ibid., 349.

[16] Ibid., 343–44.

[17] Luther, "The Babylonian Captivity," *LW* 36:51.

rests on God's promise, given by Christ and through his presence in the sacraments to each particular Christian.

God's Promise in Christ

To shed a bit more light on this, it would be helpful to turn to Luther's concept of testament. Luther locates in this term the key to grasping what happens in a sacrament, namely, God's gifts of presence and promise. Luther introduces the term as something quite ordinary and builds on it the bulk of his sacramental theology: "A testament, as everyone knows, is a promise made by one about to die, in which he designates his bequest and appoints his heirs. A testament, therefore, involves first, the death of the testator, and second, the promise of an inheritance and the naming of the heir."[18] Luther sees the concept of a testament—the promise made by one who is about to die—in the whole of the Mass. The Mass is a promise, the promise of God given to us humans in the celebration of the sacrament. This point leads to two questions: first, what is the content of this promise God gives (i.e., what is the inheritance), and, second, how does one access this promise (i.e., who are the heirs and how might one join that group)?[19] To the first point, God's promise given in Christ is for Luther the promise of salvation, which connotes for him the forgiveness of sins and life everlasting.[20] One ought not come to the sacraments looking for anything other than this. The forgiveness of sins and life everlasting are the inheritance named by Christ's testament—Christ's promise—and they are what God in Christ offers in the Mass.

This may seem an obvious point, but one ought to note some of the things Luther does *not* see as the content of the inheritance that is God's promise. Merit, for example, is not part of the promise, according to Luther (though this comes as no surprise considering his thought on the very concept of merit).[21] Neither is worldly prosperity or even security a necessary part of Luther's concept of salvation. Third and perhaps most notably, not even increase in charity or moral progress is part of God's promise of salvation. It is the forgiveness of sins and life

---

[18] Ibid., 38–39.

[19] By "how," I do not mean "where"; we are speaking here of the Sacrament of the Altar, the Eucharist. I mean, "By what mechanism, action, or attribute is God's given promise received?"

[20] Luther, "Babylonian Captivity," *LW* 36:38–40.

[21] Luther, "Ninety-Five Theses, 1517" *LW* 1:30–31.

everlasting that God offers in Christ; we humans neither can merit this nor is merit given to us, Christ's kingdom is not of this world, and forgiveness is forgiveness, not an ethical mandate.

All this is to say that what happens in the sacraments according to Luther is the gift of God's promise in Christ, the content of which is forgiveness of sins and eternal life. That is all that is received because that is what is promised; anything else added on (e.g., moral conversion, worldly justice, or increase in charity) is just that—added on without scriptural warrant and thus, for Luther, without divine warrant. In speaking of what happens in the sacraments, Luther is not concerned with speaking of what happens as a result of them, as if the sacraments and what springs from them could be somehow linked as a cause-and-effect verification of "real" reception. God's promise is of forgiveness and eternal life. We ought not to look for more than that in the sacraments themselves.

The second point—that of how one might access Christ's testament—is the familiar refrain of Lutheran theology as a whole: *sola fide*, by faith alone. All that is "required" in order to become heirs named in Christ's testament is to trust Christ's promise *that* we are heirs named in Christ's testament. This sometimes has led readers of Luther to claim that the doctrine of faith alone, far from ridding soteriology of works righteousness, instead simply boils all works down into one fundamental and necessary work: the work of faith. Luther himself at times seems ambivalent in this regard, claiming both that "faith is not a work" and that "[faith] is the most excellent and difficult of all works," even in the same treatise.[22] This is, however, an illusory ambivalence in Luther, for when he speaks of faith as a work, he quickly moves on to explain that it is neither a work in which we humans are active nor one for which we humans are responsible. One ought to keep in mind that we are still speaking of accessing Christ's testament, which is something that is given and in which an inheritance is promised. Speaking within this image, Luther maintains that there is no action to be taken on the part of the heirs; the one who *gives* the testament has done all the preparation and work. The heirs receive and do so passively:

> Who in the world is so foolish as to regard a promise received by him, or a testament given to him, as a good work, which he renders to the testator by his acceptance of it? What heir will imagine that he is doing

[22] Luther, "Babylonian Captivity," *LW* 36:47, 62.

his departed father a kindness by accepting the terms of the will and the inheritance it bequeaths to him? What godless audacity is it, therefore, when we who are to receive the testament of God come as those who would perform a good work for him![23]

For Luther, Christ's testament has nothing at all to do with our works, and speaking of faith as a good work in the context of receiving God's gift is nonsensical. Faith is "required" for reception, not as a prerequisite, but as the means for Christ's testament. It is something like a mechanism rather than a requirement. One might conceive of it this way: Faith, in Luther's view, is like one's sense of hearing, if one thinks of the testament of Christ as a gift of song. The song is not created by the hearer, nor is the hearer responsible for the song's performance or quality. Likewise, the song is only available to the hearer *via* the capacity of hearing, over which the hearer does not exercise control either positively or negatively. Hearing in this case is not a work, but it *is* required in order to access the song. Taking this a step further, one's capacity for hearing is also (in the context of the Christian worldview) a gift received from God, or at least an attribute that one did not create her- or himself. Likewise faith is a gift received from God, or at least a "work" in which humans are passive recipients rather than active agents: "Faith is a work of God, not of man, as Paul teaches [Eph 2:8]. The other works he works through us and with our help, but this one alone he works in us and without our help."[24]

At this point one might object to Luther that, while he has maintained that no works are required in order to inherit forgiveness of sins and eternal life, and also that faith itself is not a work, he has nevertheless restricted the work of God in Christ to the mechanism of faith—something that relies on participation in the sacraments, hearing preaching, or at least knowledge of the Gospel of Christ. In essence, one might claim that Luther has excised the necessity of works of love and mediation specifically by the clergy from the economy of salvation but has ignored the fact that in his alternative view of *sola fide*, what remains necessary are the *church's* works and mediation (preaching, sacraments, etc.). Put another way, one might claim that Luther has transformed works righteousness by an individual for the individual into works righteousness by the church for its members.

[23] Ibid., 47–48.
[24] Ibid., 62.

Luther himself would certainly not see his view of *sola fide* in this way. He would argue that while God indeed *does* use the tools of preaching and sacraments as means of grace, this fact does not limit God to those specific means, as if such "works" of the church are required for God to reach the church's members. For Luther, God could in fact use any means God might choose in order to reach humans. Anticipating by a few hundred years Karl Barth's claim that "God may speak to us through . . . a flute concerto, a blossoming shrub, or a dead dog,"[25] Luther maintains that,

> Although [God] is present in all creatures, and I might find him in stone, in fire, in water, or even in a rope . . . he does not wish that I seek him there apart from the Word, and cast myself into the fire or the water, or hang myself on the rope. He is present everywhere, but he does not wish that you grope for him everywhere. Grope rather where the Word is, and there you will lay hold of him in the right way.[26]

Luther's point is that God *can* give the gifts of everlasting life and forgiveness of sins in any way God chooses, but God has also given us humans the Word and sacraments as means of grace, so there is little reason to disparage those gifts. Preaching and the sacraments are for our benefit—not God's. They are not requirements but gifts in which we may access the full gifts of God's promise in Christ.

God's Presence in Christ

Beyond God's gift of the promise of the forgiveness of sins and eternal life, God also gives in the sacraments the presence of Christ. This is not unconnected from God's promises in Christ, but neither are they identical. God's promise is of forgiveness and eternal life, and Christ's presence in the sacraments (particularly in the Lord's Supper) testifies to those promises and makes them newly part of the church and its members at every celebration. In this sense Christ's presence is effective for salvation; it is not in and of itself forgiveness and eternal life, but it bears witness to those gifts and bears them to the recipients of the sacraments. Christ's presence is not a kind of magical property that is infused on the altar in order to make the Eucharist "work"; it *works* in

---

[25] Karl Barth, *Church Dogmatics* 1.1, ed. G. W. Bromiley and T. F. Torrance, trans. G. W. Bromiley (Peabody, MA: Hendrickson, 2010), 55.

[26] Luther, "Against the Fanatics," *LW* 36:342.

the Eucharist as a kind of guarantee of the promise. Christ's presence is not only salvific because of what it *is* (though that may be true as well), but also and primarily because of what it *does*: Christ's presence in the Eucharist becomes a part of the human participant, uniting the believer with Christ and thus consummating God's promise of salvation in particular human lives.

In order for such a consummation to take place, however, Luther argues that Christ's presence in the Eucharist must be real. If it is not, then neither is the believer's connection to God's promise real. Again, for Luther this is not because God *could not* adopt humans as heirs in any other way but rather because God in Christ has revealed that his presence in the Eucharist *is* real, making the Eucharist a kind of guaranteed locus of participating in God's promise of salvation. That said, the reality of Christ's presence (or lack thereof) was a question that dominated a large portion of sixteenth-century debates concerning the sacraments, and Luther weighed in on the question often. As such, it is worthwhile to summarize Luther's approach to the reality of Christ's presence here. Particularly with an eye to our discussion of Luther and Chauvet together below, clarity with regard to how Luther conceives of Christ's presence is a prerequisite to discussing sacramental presence with Chauvet. In order to approach such clarity, we look briefly at two sources: the *Babylonian Captivity*, which contains one of Luther's most sustained and systematic treatments of how Christians ought *not* to conceive of Christ's real presence in the Eucharist, and *Against the Fanatics*, which contains the reverse—how *to* conceive of Christ's presence.

Luther's problem with what had become in his time the dominant Roman Catholic way of thinking about Christ's real presence in the Eucharist (transubstantiation) was twofold: he maintained, first, that the ecclesial hierarchy at the time was attempting to make the formula of transubstantiation an article of faith and, second, that transubstantiation itself is at best unnecessarily complicated and more realistically implies an idolatry of philosophy. Luther's first objection against transubstantiation stemmed from what became another hallmark of Lutheran theology in particular and Protestant theology in general: *sola scriptura*. For Luther, "The Word of God—and no one else, not even an angel— should establish articles of faith."[27] The idea that it had become the

---

[27] Martin Luther, *The Smalclad Articles* (1537), in *The Book of Concord*, ed. Robert Kolb and Timothy J. Wengert (Minneapolis, MN: Fortress, 2000), 304.

norm to conceive of Christ's presence in the Eucharist in a way that did not, in Luther's view, come from Christ himself (meaning a way of thinking that did not come directly from scripture)—and this to the exclusion of other ways of thinking—was a grave doctrinal error for Luther. In his view, it is scripture that contains truth and the articles of faith.

To the extent that doctrines add on to the truth of scriptural revelation, they remain exactly that—add-ons—and they cannot exclude other doctrines unless those other doctrines contradict scriptural revelation. In Luther's words, "What is asserted without the Scriptures or proven revelation may be held as an opinion, but need not be believed."[28] That no council had actually made transubstantiation an article of faith made little difference to Luther; in practice, the doctrine of transubstantiation held sway in such a way that every other conception of real presence was considered heretical, and this was the problem. In practice if not in definition, transubstantiation held a doctrinal monopoly without scriptural warrant.

Luther's second objection against transubstantiation was that it was an unnecessarily complex way of conceiving of something that scripture presented rather simply. In his words, "I rejoice greatly that the simple faith of this sacrament is still to be found, at least among the common people. For they . . . believe with a simple faith that Christ's body and blood are truly contained [in the Eucharist], and leave to those who have nothing else to do the argument about what contains them."[29] Transubstantiation moves beyond this "simple" way of looking at the Eucharist and adds—according to Luther—nothing of value to sacramental theology. That it was considered the single legitimate way to speak of Christ's presence only exacerbated the matter. Further, Luther maintains that transubstantiation breaks the rules of the philosophical system on which it is based in order to become theologically and ritually acceptable, and if that is a valid step in order to move toward transubstantiation, why not also create other ways of thinking about the sacrament that break similar rules? Why is it acceptable to break some philosophical rules but not others? Luther puts one example of his frustration in this way:

[28] Luther, "Babylonian Captivity," *LW* 36:29.
[29] Ibid., 32.

Hence for [Aristotle], "this white," "this large," "this something," are all subjects, of which something is predicated. If that is correct, I ask: If a "transubstantiation" must be assumed in order that Christ's body may not be identified with the bread, why not also a "transaccidentation," in order that the body of Christ may not be identified with the accidents? For the same danger remains if one understands the subject to be "this white or this round is my body." And for the same reason that a "transubstantiation" must be assumed, a "transaccidentation" must also be assumed, because of this identity of the subject and predicate.[30]

In the end, transubstantiation is, for Luther, a shaky way of conceiving of Christ's presence in the Eucharist that is bereft of any redeeming qualities, most notably lacking scriptural warrant and philosophical consistency.[31]

Springing from these two fundamental deficiencies Luther sees in transubstantiation, Luther's second objection is also indicative of his caution with regard to philosophy in general. Much ink has been spilled on Luther and nominalism,[32] but more to the current point is Luther's disdain for Aristotle and the theological positions based on his thought. For Luther, philosophy may be used only with great care theologically, and then only to support opinions on what has been revealed in scripture, not to define articles of faith apart from scripture.[33] Luther did not maintain that no Christian should ever conceive of what happens in the Eucharist as transubstantiation. In fact, he explicitly allows for doing so: "Therefore I permit every man to hold either of these opinions, as he chooses" (denoting what Luther saw as Thomas's opinion of tran-

---

[30] Ibid., 33.

[31] Or so Luther argues: "This opinion of Thomas [transubstantiation] hangs so completely in the air without support of Scripture or reason that it seems to me he [Thomas] knows neither his philosophy nor his logic. For Aristotle speaks of subject and accidents so very differently from St. Thomas that it seems to me this great man is to be pitied not only for attempting to draw his opinions in matters of faith from Aristotle, but also for attempting to base them upon a man whom he did not understand" ("Babylonian Captivity," *LW* 36:29).

[32] See, for example, Graham White, *Luther as Nominalist: A Study of the Logical Methods Used in Martin Luther's Disputations in the Light of Their Medieval Background* (Helsinki, Finland: Luther-Agricola-Society, 1994).

[33] Interestingly, Luther does not seem to mind the insertion of the extra-scriptural term *homoousios* into the very creedal formulation of the church. Such an issue, however, runs beyond the scope of this discussion.

substantiation, on the one hand, and the opinion of Pierre d'Ailly, on the other).[34] Instead, Luther is concerned to keep theological opinions as just that, opinions meant to help Christians rather than to rule them. To the degree that transubstantiation can do this, so much the better, but the same ought to be said of other possible positions on the subject.[35] In the end for Luther, Christ's words of institution hold sway, and everything else theologically or philosophically added on is at best helpful but not necessary for faith.

This last point—that Christ's words of institution are what are ultimately central for Luther concerning Christ's presence in the Eucharist—is the springboard for Luther's positive work on conceiving of Christ's presence, especially in his treatise *Against the Fanatics*. While Luther aimed the *Babylonian Captivity* at his Roman Catholic opponents, *Against the Fanatics* is one of Luther's attempts to answer the objections of other Protestant thinkers (specifically Karlstadt and Zwingli). While Luther was no defender of the doctrine of transubstantiation, we said above that Christ's real presence is a revealed and therefore necessary truth about the Eucharist, a position Luther defended largely on the basis of the words of institution and their simple clarity:

> If these words [of institution] are not clear, I do not know how to speak German. Would I not understand, if someone were to place a roll before me and say: "take, eat, this is white bread"? Or again, "take and drink, this is a glass of wine"? Therefore when Christ says "take, eat, this is my body," even a child will understand perfectly well that he is speaking of that which he is offering. . . . For this reason we stick closely to the words and close our eyes and senses, because everyone knows what "this is my body" means, especially when [Christ] adds "given for you." We know what Christ's body is, namely, that which was born of Mary, suffered, died, and rose again.[36]

For Luther, Christ's words of institution are to be taken literally. For him, there is nothing in the gospel narratives to suggest that Christ

---

[34] Luther, "Babylonian Captivity," *LW* 36:28–30.

[35] It should be noted that Luther does not explicitly use the term "consubstantiation." Nevertheless, his explanations of how "simple faith" might conceive of the sacrament do carry a number of resonances with this position. The point remains for Luther, however, that how one conceives of Christ's presence in the Eucharist is secondary to the fact that one has faith in Christ's presence in the Eucharist.

[36] Luther, "Against the Fanatics," *LW* 36:337–38.

meant these words in any way other than the literal sense, so to inject nuance and subtleties into the words (especially at the expense of the literal meaning, the real presence) is to "suck the egg dry and leave us the shell."[37] As Luther positively conceives of Christ's eucharistic presence, his most emphatic point is simply *that* Christ is really present in the Eucharist. One ought not to make so simple a thing into a complex problem; Christ says that the Eucharist is his body and blood, so it is.

The question one might see as naturally springing from this assertion—that of exactly *how* Christ is present—Luther sees as relatively unimportant. *Against the Fanatics* is one of his most zealous writings in defense of Christ's real presence in the Eucharist, yet even in this treatise Luther constructs his explanations of how Christ is present as images rather than arguments, and then only in order to lay the groundwork for his explanations of what the sacrament is for: justification (and assurance thereof) and inspiration of the "fruits of the sacrament."[38] Luther uses many images in this work and elsewhere to represent Christ's presence in the Eucharist: the image of iron and fire simultaneously present in red-hot iron,[39] the image of the soul in the body (present in all the members simultaneously), the soul's ability to simultaneously think and speak, the ability of a single grain of wheat to produce a full stalk and head of grains, and the ability of a voice to rule a nation (as a ruler commands).[40] All of these are possible analogies for Christ's presence in the Eucharist, and they can be helpful so far as they go. The point of these analogies, however, is not to become stuck in exactly how to conceive of Christ's presence but to be able to receive Christ *as* really present. Images of Christ's eucharistic presence (or models, or philosophical constructions) serve as something of a bridge for Luther, between the fact *that* Christ is really present on the one hand, and the *purposes* of Christ's presence on the other.

The purpose of Christ's presence is the point toward which Luther moves his audience in *Against the Fanatics* and the point that will finally help this discussion to move from Luther's sacramental theology into how Luther views the connection between sacraments and ethics. In his words, "It is not sufficient that we know what the sacrament is, namely, that Christ's body and blood are truly present, but it is also necessary

---

[37] Ibid., 336.
[38] Ibid., 350–52.
[39] Luther, "Babylonian Captivity," *LW* 36:32.
[40] Luther, "Against the Fanatics," *LW* 36:338–39.

to know why they are present and for what reason they are given to us to be received."[41] For Luther, this "why" of the sacraments is profound; it is "the whole Christian doctrine," which Luther explains as two principles: what a Christian is to believe and what a Christian is to do.[42] The first principle—what a Christian is to believe—we have already discussed at length in this section: the Christian is to believe in God's saving gifts of promise and presence. The first principle of Christian doctrine for Luther, then, is justification ("that Christ has given his body, flesh, and blood on the cross to be our treasure and to help us to receive forgiveness of sins, that is, that we may be saved, redeemed from death and hell"[43]), and this is the first "why" of sacraments for him. Sacraments help Christians to receive justification. Nevertheless, to reiterate briefly a point we've been consistently making, this reception is not a work done by humans. We humans receive forgiveness of sins and eternal life, but we do so in faith, which is a work of God in us and for us. Additionally, this does not mean justification is infused without mundane aids either.[44] What Christ gave once and for all time on the cross we humans receive once in baptism and repeatedly in the Eucharist: Christ's very self, which bears witness to his promise, and in which we humans are named heirs to forgiveness of sins and life everlasting.

For Luther, this first principle of Christian doctrine, which humans also access through the Word in preaching, comes in the sacraments specifically to discrete individual humans. As we alluded to above, this is one of the ways Luther distinguishes between Christ's presence in the Word and Christ's presence in the sacraments. Says Luther:

> When I preach [Christ's] death, it is in a public sermon in the congregation, in which I am addressing myself to no one individually; whoever grasps it, grasps it. But when I distribute the sacrament, I designate it for the individual who is receiving it; I give [him or her] Christ's body and blood that [he or she] may have forgiveness of sins, obtained through his death and preached in the congregation.[45]

---

[41] Ibid., 347.

[42] Ibid., 352.

[43] Ibid.

[44] One might claim the contrary here and cite "forensic justification" as exactly this kind of infusion of justification. I will return to this claim below, but at this point in the discussion it suffices that Luther does not exclude sacramental mediation of justification; he endorses it.

[45] Luther, "Against the Fanatics," *LW* 36:348.

In Luther's view, what is distributed to the community *qua* community by preaching is distributed to the individuals of the community in the sacraments (especially the Eucharist). In this way, no participating member of the congregation can "miss" Christ's presence, and the sacraments drive home that salvation—the first principle of Christian doctrine—is given to each person as a unique "you."[46] It is not required of each person to grasp Christ's presence in the preached word (though that is, of course, a good thing if it happens); Christ's saving presence also comes to each person in the Eucharist so that, once again, salvation depends in no way on the abilities or faculties of the humans being saved. This assurance of salvation, together with salvation itself, is the first principle of "the whole Christian doctrine," and it is the inspiration for the second principle, which for Luther is love.[47]

Without immediately diving too deeply into how Luther's first principle of Christian doctrine inspires the second (this will be the subject of the remainder of this chapter), it would nevertheless be helpful to understand what exactly Luther means here by love. In the first place, this second principle—love—comes to us humans as an example to be emulated. While Luther certainly had problems with the concept of *imitatio Christi*, and that idea has had a rocky history in Lutheran theology ever since, Luther still maintains that we humans receive, along with justification and assurance thereof, an example in the sacraments (especially the Eucharist):

> As [Christ] gives himself to us with his body and blood in order to redeem us from all misery, so we too are to give ourselves with might and main for our neighbor. Whoever knows this and lives accordingly is holy, and has not much more to learn, nor will he find anything more in the whole Bible.[48]

To love one's neighbor as Christ has loved us is the second principle of Luther's "whole of Christian doctrine." Notice, however, that in this context—namely, the context of justification rather than condemnation, or the context of gospel rather than law—this principle Luther calls an example rather than a mandate or even a commandment. Elsewhere Luther does, of course, speak of Christ's command to "love each other

[46] Ibid., 348–49.
[47] Ibid., 352.
[48] Ibid.

as I have loved you,"[49] but what Christians receive in the sacraments are justification and Christ's example of love, *not* any requirements or "strings attached." What Christians receive in the sacraments remains the utterly free gift of God, with no conditions (so far as salvation is concerned) that it leads to anything beyond Christian reception of the gifts.

This section has outlined the core points of Luther's sacramental theology. It began by echoing Luther's insistence that the sacraments are actions taken by God rather than works done by humans. In the sacraments, God gives. Specifically, God gives gifts of divine promises and presence. The promises of God in Christ—Christ's testament—are the promises of forgiveness of sins and life everlasting, which humans receive by faith alone. Even faith itself is not a work done by humans but is an action by God within and on behalf of the human. The section then moved on to discuss the way Luther views the presence of Christ in the sacraments, specifically his problems with transubstantiation and his emphasis that the real presence of Christ is salvific (it justifies humans) and reassuring (it testifies to God's promises, aiding faith and connecting God's promises to each individual believer). Finally, this section has ended by exploring briefly what Luther sees as the purpose of sacraments, namely, that they effect both justification and love, which together are for Luther the entirety of Christian doctrine. Having accomplished this, chapter 2 now turns explicitly to how Luther conceives of that second principle—love—as connected to and inspired by the first principle, justification.

Sacraments and Ethics as Union with Christ

This section will argue that, for Luther, love is always consequent upon faith and justification, and therefore a correct understanding of Christian love and ethics depends on a correct understanding of sin, faith, justification, and sanctification. As such, this section begins with a summary of Luther's view of the human predicament of sin, along with the way he conceives of works. Building on this, the section moves to what justification and sanctification include for Luther, centered on his concept of the Christian as *simul iustus et peccator*. The *simul* provides a way of bridging the gap between what happens in justification, namely,

---

[49] See Martin Luther, *Sermons on the Gospel of John*, LW 24:248–51.

the unification of the believer with Christ (again, taking as our herme-neutic the Finnish School), and sanctification, the life of the human after justification. By lifting up the concept of union with Christ, I do not mean to deny the value of viewing justification as divinely imputed. Such an interpretation has a long and celebrated history in Lutheran theology, and it is helpful so far as it goes. Emphasizing union with Christ in faith, however, rather than the externally imputed nature of justification allows this discussion to move more directly into conversa-tion with Chauvet on sacraments and ethics, without losing emphasis on Luther's core insights. Having sketched this summary, the section moves to a deeper consideration of what sanctification looks like in Christian life for Luther and how exactly this relates justification (wrought in the believer by God's grace in the sacraments) to ethics (made possible by the continuing grace of Christ present in faith).

Two Kinds of Works, and Two Kinds of Righteousness

For Luther, the human lives life as a sinner rightly deserving con-demnation, and, as a result, all human works are in a certain sense, as acts before God perpetrated by a sinner, actually sins.[50] Before even beginning to consider justification and sanctification, one must realize that everything a human does before justification is sinful, even what humans might see as admirable works. This means that, for Luther, sin covers the entirety of human existence; sin is *not* the same as immorality, and neither is it simply the opposite of following the law. Sin is the state of humanity as out of right relationship with God, and it is renewed by every human action *as* the action of one who is out of right relationship. One might think of this situation as analogous to a broken friendship. If one loses a friend by perpetrating some heinous act (dare we say, an "original sin"), then that friendship is ruptured. This is hardly profound on its own, but then imagine the guilty friend attempts to mend the friendship by engaging in activities both friends used to share together. The trouble is, these actions are now tainted by the shadow of the heinous act that ruptured the friendship in the first place, which con-stitutes, in Luther's words, "heaping sins upon sins."[51] Far from healing the friendship, each new act actually drives the friends further apart, because the guilty friend does not realize that forgiveness cannot be

---

[50] Luther, *Lectures on Galatians, 1535*, LW 26:126.
[51] Ibid.

earned in this way. This is doubly tragic, because not only can new actions not "undo" the rupture but they actually reinforce the rupture, renewing its poison precisely *because* of the presence of that rupture they attempt to undo.

Given this backdrop of sin, Luther adopts something of a dual language with regard to works.[52] Roughly speaking, he uses the term "works of the law" to indicate works that are in accord with the law. These can belong to the entirety of humankind, as Luther points not only to Peter and Paul as exemplars of working according to the law but also to Xenophon, Cicero, Pomponius, and others.[53] Luther's point is that works of the law have nothing to do with justification or faith. They constitute what Luther calls "active righteousness," or a kind of righteousness that is, strictly speaking, still hobbled by sin. Works of the law, precisely because they are works springing from the law rather than the gospel, for Luther then also help to fulfill the law's purpose: demonstrating to us humans our weakness and sinfulness. To conceive of works of the law as somehow positive or (especially) meritorious is nonsensical for Luther, because that would lead also to claiming that doing works of the law ought to be rewarded, putting God in the debt of sinners.[54] Instead, works of the law are "good" only insofar as the law itself is "good," meaning that they help the sinner to "first acknowledge, through the law, that [he or she] *is* a sinner, for whom it is impossible to perform any good work."[55]

The term "works of the law" represents one half of Luther's dual language on works, while "good works" represents the other. Good works are works of love springing from faith and therefore have everything to do with justification and Christ's action (though, of course, not as prerequisites). Good works do not carry the taint of sin but neither are they meritorious, because the faith from which they spring is the faith of Christ, and the active agent is Christ-in-us rather than we humans ourselves. Good works may outwardly appear exactly the same

---

[52] I say "something of a dual language" only to indicate that Luther's language is not completely consistent in this usage. He is not a systematic theologian. Nevertheless, I include this distinction because I believe it will help clarify how Luther conceives of the drama of salvation, namely, the problem of sin, rectified in justification, the act of which inspires Christian love and the good works that constitute it.

[53] Luther, "Lectures on Galatians, 1535," *LW* 26:123–24.

[54] Ibid., 124.

[55] Ibid., 125, 126. Emphasis added.

as works of the law, but their motivation is different; in fact, the agent is different. "Works of the law," says Luther, "can be performed either before justification or after justification,"[56] but good works are the action of Christ within the justified sinner. Luther holds this together with the formula *simul iustus et peccator*: we Christians are and continue to be sinners, and insofar as that is the case, our works of the law are still colored by sin. Christians are, however, also justified, meaning that Christ acts in us and that our works, born of faith, are also good works. This *simul* is central to Luther's logic of sin and redemption, and in order to appreciate how it helps inform the connection of sacraments and ethics, we now turn to Luther's concept of justification and dual language of righteousness.

If no human action can undo sin, nor can the human actively do anything except sin, then justification in Luther's view is utterly passive on the part of the human and is completely a result of God's action on our behalf. For Luther, justification is the believer's passive reception of Christian righteousness.[57] While this axiom does not appear word-for-word in Luther, it captures a good degree of his emphasis (especially in his commentaries on Galatians). As Luther has a dual language of works, so he has a dual language of righteousness, namely, a language of Christian righteousness, on the one hand, and of active righteousness, on the other. One might think of works of the law as associated with active righteousness and good works as springing from—though never constituting—Christian righteousness. What Luther means by Christian righteousness is, quite literally, Christ-in righteousness, or the righteousness of Christ. (He treats a number of other phrases as synonyms of this term, such as "heavenly righteousness," "eternal righteousness," "righteousness of grace."[58]) As such, it cannot be in any way produced or cultivated by humans, because it is received in utter passivity. Luther likens this Christian righteousness to rain falling on the earth:

> As the earth itself does not produce rain and is unable to acquire it by its own strength, worship, and power but receives it only by a heavenly gift from above, so this heavenly righteousness is given to us by God without our work or merit. As much as the dry earth of itself is able to accomplish in obtaining the right and blessed rain, that much can we

---

[56] Ibid., 123.
[57] Ibid., 8.
[58] Ibid., 6.

[humans] accomplish by our own strength and works to obtain that divine, heavenly, and eternal righteousness. Thus we can obtain it only through the free imputation and indescribable gift of God.[59]

This point—that Christian righteousness is a gift from God—separates for Luther this kind of righteousness that is salvific and eternal from all other kinds of righteousness that are earthly, temporal, and have nothing to do with salvation. The familiar Lutheran dichotomy of law and gospel rings true in Luther's treatment of righteousness; just as the gospel is heavenly, a gift, and can only be received, so is Christian righteousness heavenly, a gift, and only to be received. Likewise, active righteousness—what Luther also calls righteousness according to the law—is earthly and has dominion over the flesh in the same way the law is and does.[60] These two kinds of righteousness do not inform one another for Luther, nor do they even come into contact. There is a real separation between these two, almost to the point of opposition (again, not unlike the separation between law and gospel, or the duality of works of the law and good works). For Luther, Christian righteousness is not active righteousness, and active righteousness does not aid or inhibit Christian righteousness. In Luther's words, "Between these two kinds of righteousness . . . there is no middle ground."[61]

Lest this appear to suggest that Luther has no real place for active righteousness, one ought to note that the law for Luther—which is the basis both for active righteousness and works of the law—is "holy, righteous, and good."[62] It has its purposes, but it is to be kept separate from questions of salvation and justification. If one can indeed disconnect active righteousness from justification, then two roles for this righteousness according to the law become apparent. First, active righteousness has the purpose of cultivating works of the law. It is the realm of the "ought." We humans ought to love God and neighbor, ought to honor our father and mother, ought to keep the Lord's Day holy, and so

[59] Ibid.

[60] I do not mean here "earthly" as if somehow the law and active righteousness are authored only by humans. I use "earthly" here to indicate that the effects of this righteousness—and the law—do not extend for Luther beyond Earth and creation into salvation and the eschaton.

[61] Martin Luther, "Lectures on Galatians, 1535," *LW* 26:9.

[62] Ibid., 123.

on.[63] Luther takes pains to point out this necessity of righteousness according to the law, "in order that no one may suppose that we reject or prohibit good works."[64] Works of the law are "good" things for Luther; they just belong to active righteousness rather than to Christian righteousness. Simply put, they are *works*. They are not unnecessary or irrelevant or useless to the human; they are just separate from faith and salvation and fulfill a role that has nothing to do with faith or salvation. Works of the law are good for the flesh and the old human; they just have no bearing for good or ill on the spirit and the new human.

Second, righteousness according to the law serves to illuminate for Christians their own sinfulness. For Luther, the law itself "only shows sin, terrifies, and humbles; thus it prepares us for justification and drives us to Christ."[65] Consequently, active righteousness will only ever be incomplete for humans; humans by their own power cannot fulfill the law. When one comprehends the law, according to Luther, one can only realize that one is a sinner and worthy of damnation. At this point one can see the slight difference in Luther's thought between works of the law (works that anyone can do sometimes or even often, either intentionally or unintentionally, but that cannot ultimately fulfill the law) and active righteousness. Works of the law do not in and of themselves reveal oneself as a sinner; they are discrete actions in accord with the law that help the law as a whole to reveal the human as sinner. Active righteousness, however, is that "entirety" of the law of which humans always fall short. Active righteousness can be had partially but never fully, since one can act according to the law partially but cannot fulfill it. In this way, for Luther, active righteousness "crushes" the old human—the flesh—leaving it "accused, exercised, saddened."[66] The law condemns humans, because full active righteousness is unattainable for us sinful creatures. Luther calls this realization—this knowledge of oneself as rightly damned—"the first step in Christianity."[67]

---

[63] Luther lumps together both the moral and ceremonial aspects of the law, as he claims Paul does: "For Paul 'works of the law' means the works of the entire law. Therefore one should not make a distinction between the Decalog and ceremonial laws" (Luther, "Lectures on Galatians, 1535," *LW* 26:122).

[64] Luther, "Lectures on Galatians, 1535," *LW* 26:7.

[65] Ibid., 126.

[66] Ibid., 9.

[67] Ibid., 126. Like faith, though, one should not read this as an epiphany the human reaches by his or her own natural powers. The law is of God, and *every* "step" in Christianity is God's work.

If Luther's first step in Christianity is the knowledge that one is a sinner, then the second step is God's saving action. (This is not to suggest God's action comes after humans' knowledge; God is active even in humans' realization of their sinfulness.) This is the point at which active righteousness can have Christian righteousness added on to it. As Luther explains,

> The law only shows sin, terrifies, and humbles; thus it prepares us for justification and drives us to Christ. For by His Word God has revealed to us that He wants to be a merciful Father to us. Without our merit—since, after all, we cannot merit anything—He wants to give us forgiveness of sins, righteousness, and eternal life for the sake of Christ. For God is He who dispenses His gifts freely to all, and this is the praise of His deity. . . . This, in summary, is our theology about Christian righteousness.[68]

Christian righteousness is then added on to the active righteousness of the law, and the human (now justified) becomes capable of good works. Or put another way, Christ now dwells within the human, united with the human in faith, so good works can flow from this newfound freedom from sin. From the outside, good works and works of the law look the same—in fact, in many cases they are the same actions—but the distinction between them is that a good work is inspired by faith, while a work of the law can be the result of any number of earthly drives, desires, or convictions. I've been drawing this distinction between good works and works of the law a good deal more starkly than Luther himself does, but the reason for this is that understanding the difference (as well as the difference between active righteousness and Christian righteousness) can help illuminate what Luther means by the human as *simul iustus et peccator*.

The Bridge to Ethics: Luther's *Simul*

The central point of Luther's *simul* is this: good works and works of the law, grace and sin, and active righteousness and Christian righteousness are all present in the human simultaneously. God's saving action, in light of the *simul*, does not necessarily move the Christian *from* one state to another state. In Luther's thought, God's action in and on behalf of Christ *adds* or imputes Christ's righteousness onto/into the sinful human, creating something new, but only in the sense that the human

---

[68] Luther, "Lectures on Galatians, 1535," *LW* 26:126–27.

is still now who he or she always was *and* is also justified. Unification with Christ, having Christ present in faith, does not mean for Luther that humans are "cleansed" from their old sinful ways. They are reborn united with Christ, and yet with their old selves still constantly tugging at them.

One might (nearly correctly, I think) argue at this point that Luther has a somewhat schizophrenic theological anthropology. In light of the *simul*, there are very nearly two identities in the human person: one who is justified by faith and united with Christ and one who is sinful and damned. While this is not too far from the truth, Luther's own conception in the *simul* is not to split the human into two separate persons but to reckon honestly with human life as a fusion between flesh and spirit.[69] This last duality to which we turn encapsulates all those we've mentioned thus far. For Luther, the flesh is the realm of the law, works of the law, active righteousness, sin, and damnation, while the spirit is the realm of faith, Christian righteousness, good works (at least as I've outlined them above), and freedom from the law. Luther's *simul* is his way of conceiving of how these two realms interact. They are both present in the human and exercise influence on the human's actions to a greater or lesser extent. This is not a theological deduction for Luther; it is an analysis of what Christian life looks like. The Christian is justified, to be sure, so the Christian is freed from the condemnation of the law and freed *for* good works. Christ present in the faith of the justified believer makes good works possible. Christian experience attests, however, to the fact that sin and the desires and weaknesses of the flesh linger within the person, pulling him or her back into sin and despair over salvation.[70] Christian life then plays out as the struggle to navigate this dual life of spirit and flesh in what is actually a single, unified existence.

This struggle of Christian life is the lens through which this discussion's attention now turns to outline a model of ethics in Luther, namely, that of ethics as Christ-in-us. Luther himself does not often use the term "ethics," so any definition adopted here will be at least slightly

---

[69] For a sustained treatment of Luther's *simul*, see Wilhelm Weber, *Simul Iustus et Peccator: Die Anthropologie der Rechtfertigungslehre Luthers* (Norderstedt, Germany: GRIN Verlag, 2013), or Gary A. Mann, *Simul Iustus et Peccator: Luther's Paradigm of the Christian Life and Systematic Principle* (PhD diss., Drew University, 1988).

[70] Luther's commentary on Romans 7 is most instructive for this. See Martin Luther, *Lectures on Romans*, LW 25:322–43.

anachronistic. Nevertheless, in order to more easily facilitate the dialogue between Luther and Chauvet (the subject of the fourth chapter below), I will take ethics to connote in Luther what it seems to in Chauvet, namely, the set of actions of a person's life in the world.[71] I do not mean by this definition that every action a person takes is *de facto* ethical; I mean that every action a person takes has an ethical component (admittedly, to varying degrees—ketchup versus mustard is perhaps less of an ethical issue than one's voting decisions, financial priorities, etc.). Beyond synergizing with Chauvet's use of the term "ethics," this definition has an affinity with Luther's hesitancy to speak of any theological concept systematically. Luther is much more interested in developing his theology in relation to discrete theological conversations and sections of scripture than he is in making certain the entirety of his thought is utterly consistent with itself. Accordingly, what I call ethics in Luther is neither a system of morality nor a set of ethical precepts; I take it to mean the set of actions held together as the whole human (ethical) life.

Within Luther's vocabulary, this definition of ethics encompasses three terms discussed thus far: active righteousness, works of the law, and good works. Recall that none of these terms has any justifying efficacy, but their relationships to justification are not necessarily the same. Works of the law and active righteousness are aspects of human life that precede justification and also endure afterward; they are the realms of the flesh for Luther.[72] Human ethical actions—the entirety of which I have called ethics—are in this sense as much non-Christian as Christian. Any moral codes, to the partial degree to which they fulfill the law, can be ethical and can legitimately prescribe works of the law and active righteousness. Christianity does not have a monopoly on ethics (or ethical reasoning) for Luther.

In this light, ethics on its own does not have any intrinsic connection to liturgy or sacraments (or even revelation) in Luther's thought. That lack of connection feeds directly into Luther's greater points about sin and justification: any connection between Word and sacrament, on the one hand, and human ethics/life, on the other, is the result not of a connection in human nature or reason but a result of the gratuitous action of God—namely, the action of God in uniting the believer with Christ. By God's word in the law, humans see themselves truthfully as

---

[71] That this is what Chauvet means by ethics is discussed in chapter 3.
[72] Luther, "Lectures on Galatians, 1535," *LW* 26:6–9.

they are: sinners who cannot fulfill the law's demands. Having been condemned by the law and active righteousness, the human then receives Christian righteousness through faith (God's work and action), and what was ethics becomes what can now properly be called "Christian ethics." To be clear, ethics may not look objectively any different from specifically Christian ethics. In fact, Luther points out that Christian life before and after justification looks identical to the outside observer: "A Christian uses the world and all its creatures in such a way that there is no difference between [him or her] and an ungodly [person]. Their food and clothing are the same; their hearing, vision, and speaking are the same; their gestures, appearance, and shape are the same."[73]

The difference between ethics and Christian ethics, then, is not in the content of one's actions but in one's relationship with God (and, therefore, according to Luther, in the reasons or inspiration behind one's actions). Before justification, one's ethical actions—works of the law—are still the actions of a sinner who is rightfully condemned by the law (whether or not the sinner realizes this). Such actions—ethics—can have no impact either positively or negatively on one's relationship with or standing before God. The human is condemnable, but in Luther's thought, sinning further will not make the person "more" condemnable, any more than acting according to the law can undo one's sinful state. Luther would still say that ethics remains important before justification, however, because the flesh—which is ruled by sin—is the province of the law, which appropriately ought to rule a person's actions (even though no person can ever fulfill it). In the flesh, human laws, moral codes, reason, and tastes can approximate the divine law, but ethics remains separate from justification—and therefore from liturgy/sacraments—by the sinful state of the flesh.

For Luther, since the flesh is ruled by sin (or enslaved to sin), ethics is colored by human sinfulness. Reason is twisted, desires and passions turn humans in on themselves, and fear of punishment plagues the conscience. Still, reason and fear are, for Luther, the sources of ethics in the human before justification. This form of ethics radically changes, however, when the sinner recognizes both that the law condemns him or her, on the one hand, and that he or she cannot by any works of the law undo that condemnation, on the other. At that point, as the rest of Christian revelation reaches the sinner, he or she also (by God's grace)

---

[73] Ibid., 171.

recognizes God's action in Christ on his or her behalf and takes hold of Christ's promise of salvation—and Christ himself—in the act of faith (which, as we said above, is ultimately God's work and not the human's).

In Luther's view, one can conceive of this move from condemnation to faith as the beginning of Christ's indwelling of the Christian. Thus far we have spoken of Christian righteousness as being "added on" to the person in justification. While this is accurate, Luther also argues that Christian righteousness ultimately is not a static entity or character but the presence of Christ himself. Just as Christ is present in Word and Sacrament, and as that presence effects and testifies to the person's justification through faith, so is Christ also present in faith itself. Faith is not only a work of God present in the human person but also the second person of the Trinity present in the human. As Luther articulates: "It is Christ who forms and trains faith or who is the form of faith. Therefore the Christ who is grasped by faith and who lives in the heart is the true Christian righteousness."[74]

This claim of Luther's is the basis for much of the Finnish School of Luther Interpretation, as we discussed in chapter 1 above; accordingly, what follows in this model of ethics is at least loosely framed by the insights of the Finnish School. In Luther's thought, the way one might conceive of Christ present in faith parallels Christ present in the sacraments. In the sacraments (particularly in the Eucharist) Christ is not present as a character or mode or accident; Christ is present substantially—though Luther would not appreciate that word—that is, in a way that is real and essential to the sacrament, because Christ's words "this is my body" and so on are to be taken in the simplest, literal sense.[75] Likewise in faith, Christ's presence is not simply a reflection of Christ or a Christ-like character, as if the once-sinful human has now been changed into a different, sinless form. Instead, Christ present in faith for Luther really means Christ, the second person of the Trinity, present in the faith of the human person.[76] In faith, the human participates in the life of God, because God in Christ lives in the human person by faith. In a sense, the believer who was the old human has put on Christ and become a Christ to others.[77]

---

[74] Ibid., 130.

[75] Luther, "The Babylonian Captivity," *LW* 36:34–35.

[76] Luther, "Lectures on Galatians, 1535," *LW* 26:129.

[77] Martin Luther, "The Freedom of a Christian," *LW* 31:351, 367.

One ought not to read Luther as claiming that Christ's presence actually changes anything intrinsic to the human in him- or herself. When Christ is taken on in faith, the human moves only from *peccator* to *simul iustus et peccator*. This is a change not of the human person but of the human's standing before God (or of the human's relationship with God). It is a change by addition rather than a change by transformation. When the believer is united with Christ, an entirely new aspect of the human becomes real, namely, the human as someone in and through whom Christ lives. Luther's purpose in developing this theology of Christ really present in faith is to answer his view of the Roman Catholic conception of "faith formed by love." According to Luther, the prevailing Roman Catholic notion of justification at his time was that faith indeed justifies, but it only justifies if it is formed by love (*fides charitate formata*).[78] For Luther, this represents a misunderstanding both of faith and of love as they are presented in the gospels and in Paul. The object of faith, as Luther reads the scriptures, is Christ alone, which makes Christ also the form of faith.[79] Before any questions of love enter the conversation concerning justification, one must, Luther maintains, realize that "faith in Christ alone justifies. . . . If faith yields on this point, the death of the Son of God will be in vain."[80] Luther does not entertain questions of what this faith looks like, or what is required for this faith, or how one embodies this faith, because as we said above, this justifying faith is not a work of the human but a work of God in Christ. Christ present in faith really means that justification has absolutely nothing to do with how we think or act but rather with how God acts within us. The human receives Christian faith as the action of God in Christ, whose presence *is* the Christian righteousness received through faith.

While Luther is clear that faith is God's work, that Christ is truly present in faith, and that the love that springs from such Christian faith is divine love, the *simul* still dominates his theological anthropology.

---

[78] Luther, "Lectures on Galatians, 1535," *LW* 26:88. See also Thomas Aquinas, *Summa Theologiae*, II–II, q. 4, art. 3. Whether or not Luther's reading of Thomas is accurate is not the point here; nevertheless, it is worthwhile to note where Luther sees the seeds of the problem: not simply in popular Catholicism, but in Thomas himself.

[79] Luther, "Lectures on Galatians, 1535," *LW* 26:89, 129–30. See also Mannermaa, *Christ Present in Faith*, 26–27.

[80] Luther, "Lectures on Galatians, 1535," *LW* 26:90.

There is a wealth of divine presence in the Christian righteousness that the human receives, but the sinful human is still the one who receives it. Justification does not change the human him- or herself but rather adds on Christian righteousness to the sinful human. In justification, then, Christ present in faith changes both the relationship between the sinful human and God and (consequently) also the reason and inspiration behind the human's actions. While the human is and remains a sinner, the sinner is by faith justified and freed from slavery to sin and death. This means for Luther that while the flesh remains and sinful desires still taint human reason and drives, the human conscience is liberated from its condemnation by the law and elevated above the law into the gospel message, the realm of spirit. In Luther, this is the key difference between what I have called works of the law and good works: the liberty of the human conscience by justification.[81] One might think of the difference as the distinction between "ought" and "delight"; the human ought to act according to the law but cannot fulfill that requirement because the flesh is ruled by sin. Once the human (and the conscience) is freed from sin in justification, however, and the spirit and gospel are added to the human in faith, the conscience is freed to delight in works of the law, now rightly called good works. Such works are "good" not because they are objectively different works from works of the law—in fact they are the very same works; rather, they are different because they are inspired by faith, Christ-in-us.

While works of the law become good works and yet remain works of the law, Luther's *simul* keeps other realms of human existence distinct from each other, each with its own proper governance and members. The human is now a justified sinner, a dual citizen of the world of spirit and the world of the flesh. The world of spirit and gospel is the rightful place of faith, justification, freedom, Christian ethics, and the Christian conscience for Luther. The world of the flesh holds sin and temptation, death, active righteousness, and the law. The human is a member of both realms, and human life plays out as the struggle to navigate the two. The Christian, *simul iustus et peccator*, is for Luther a creature of dichotomies. Sin and grace, law and gospel, conscience and temptation, and even human and divine all crowd each other in Christian life. The justified human really participates in the life of God, but the sinful human still struggles under the law and falls into sin.

[81] Luther, "The Freedom of a Christian," *LW* 31:350–68.

Sanctification: Getting Used to Being Justified

Thus far we have been speaking of justification and works in Luther, with only a nod to Christian ethics itself. In the sacraments the salvation accomplished by Christ through his passion, death, and resurrection becomes a part of the lives of individual believers through God's act of justification, and while in that justification the believer is united with Christ, such that Christ now works through the believer to produce good works, the question of how such a relationship actually looks for the entirety of a Christian life remains open. This is at least partially intentional; Luther's *simul* is crafted in such a way as to emphasize the discontinuities and struggles of human life as a believer who is united with Christ and yet remains sinful. Given this, Luther's thought (and Lutheran theology more generally) tends to become a bit strained or even uncomfortable in speaking of sanctification, which can sometimes be taken to mean a process by which the Christian undergoes a kind of spiritual (and/or moral) development or growth.

Sanctification in Luther, however, has precious little to do with spiritual or moral growth. For Luther, sanctification is the name given to living as justified. It is not outside justification, nor is it an appendix to justification, nor is it a progressive completion or perfecting of justification. To sanctify is for Luther "nothing else than to bring us to the Lord Christ to receive his blessing, which we could not obtain by ourselves."[82] Sanctification—making us Christians holy—Luther takes as the subject of the third article of the creed. It is not about growth in relationship with Christ but rather the entire process by which the Holy Spirit works to unite us with Christ's justifying presence. The holy catholic church, the communion of saints, the forgiveness of sins, and the resurrection of the body—all these are for Luther what sanctification includes. To be fair, Luther does speak of *holiness* as "growing daily,"[83] but he does so in the context of explaining that such holiness has nothing to do with our action or growth but rather God's action on our behalf as the Holy Spirit through the church and justification. In this way, even when speaking of sanctification, the *simul* provides Luther's theological-anthropological foundation. To be made holy by union with Christ is to have Christ added onto one's sinful existence.

---

[82] Martin Luther, *The Large Catechism*, trans. Robert H. Fischer (Philadelphia: Fortress, 1959), 59–60.

[83] Ibid., 62.

One way to think of this Christian life is to consider that there are two wills active in the Christian person, much like Christ himself had two wills—one human and one divine—but was only one person. In Christ, of course, the two wills were in harmony, while in Christian life the will of the sinful old human constantly struggles against what is Christ's divine will given in justification. Likewise, the justified human participates in two natures: the sinful human nature of which he or she is a part and the divine nature of Christ given to the human through faith. This is not to say that Christians *are* both human and divine of themselves but rather that they *participate* in both the human and divine natures by the grace of God in Christ.[84] One ought to note that in Luther's nearly dualistic theological anthropology, no part of human life rightly belongs to both the realm of the flesh and the realm of the spirit—not even the human conscience, which bears on this discussion as we consider Christian ethics.

For Luther, the Christian conscience rightly belongs to Christ and the spirit,[85] so struggles of conscience indicate a falling of the conscience back into the realm of the flesh, as the conscience either concerns itself with discerning right and wrong or despairs over its inability to do the right.[86] Luther's insistence in this regard springs from the fact that the conscience remains the *human* conscience (even if it is elevated to the spirit), which cannot on its own perfectly will the good. This is the importance of Christ present in faith; it is faith—by Christ's presence— that "directs" the conscience, or liberates the human to delight in the good. In Luther's conception, this is not so much a struggle as it is a kind of consent to the passivity of Christian righteousness. Participating in the divine life—in the divine nature—means for Luther allowing Christ to act within us. Humans remain sinful, such that any actions they take are likewise sinful. Christ is added on to humans in faith, however, so acting out of Christian love is a passive exercise rather than an active one. Active Christian ethics, for Luther, would be a contradiction in terms; the only thing humans can actively do is sin.

---

[84] Thus the conversation the Finnish School has worked to cultivate with the Eastern concept of *theosis.* Tuomo Mannermaa, "Justification and *Theosis* in Lutheran-Orthodox Perspective," in *Union with Christ: The New Finnish Interpretation of Luther,* ed. Carl E. Braaten and Robert W. Jensen (Grand Rapids, MI: Wm. B. Eerdmans, 1998), 42–69.

[85] Luther, "Lectures on Galatians, 1535," *LW* 26:11.

[86] Ibid., 35–36.

In terms of sanctification, this passivity of Christian ethics means that growth in holiness essentially includes, in Gerhard Forde's terms, "getting used to justification."[87] This is the import of sacraments for sanctification in Luther. In baptism we are buried with Christ and rise united with him in faith and new life, and yet at the same time, "we are in sin until the end of our life."[88] As Christian life unfolds, this "drowning" of the old human happens daily, as does the rising with Christ.[89] Likewise, justification takes place again and again at the Eucharist, because never is the human freed ultimately from sin until the resurrection. Unification with Christ, therefore, is a kind of surrender to allowing Christ to act through us sinful humans, even as the old human remains susceptible to sin. This is the connection of sacraments to ethics in Luther: the Holy Spirit in the sacraments unites us to Christ, whose righteousness justifies us and whose presence in faith moves us to good works and Christian ethics. Sanctification is the name Luther gives to the entirety of this process, which can happen from beginning to end again and again in human life. Life as *simul iustus et peccator* is a continual cycle of death and rebirth, but that does not mean it is stagnant; in Luther's words, "to progress is always to begin again."[90]

In a sense, Luther's view of Christian ethics is that the Christian is justified by faith and then "ought" to do whatever comes naturally (or, more correctly, what comes supernaturally). One should note that this is markedly different from the nominalist idea of "do what is in one," which is an ethics based on the idea that what is in one is ultimately good.[91] For Luther, what is in the human is ultimately a sinful nature, to the point that any action inspired or driven by human nature is damnable sin.[92] Conversely, when Christ in faith dwells within the human, good works can spring from Christ's saving presence. The active party in such a case is Christ himself, living within the justified human alongside the human's still sinful self. As I mentioned above, the Christian life is then composed of two "competing" wills: the sinful human will and Christ's sinless will. This is the implication of the passivity of Chris-

[87] See Gerhard O. Forde, "A Lutheran View of Sanctification," in *Christian Spirituality: Five Views of Sanctification* (Grove, IL: IVP, 1988), 13–15.

[88] Luther, *Lectures on Romans, LW* 25:308.

[89] Luther, *The Small Catechism*, 360.

[90] Luther, *Lectures on Romans, LW* 25:478.

[91] Gerhard O. Forde, *Justification by Faith*, 42.

[92] Ibid.

tian righteousness for Christian ethics in Luther: anything the human does actively is sin, since any active work by the human is the human will asserting itself over against Christ's divine will now present in the human. If the human will can consent to be passive in the presence of Christ, however, the human conscience is freed from the demands of active righteousness in order to delight in the good works consequent upon passive Christian righteousness.

It is true that the human will still miss the mark and fall into sin occasionally—or often—but such is the situation of living as the old human, now justified. Additionally, these sins that come after justification cannot undo God's work of justification; as Luther points out, "Christ was given . . . not for one or two sins but for all sins,"[93] and there is no reason to think that sins committed after justification are not included by this statement. It is in this light that Luther's oft-cited line makes sense: "Be a sinner, and sin boldly, but believe and rejoice in Christ even more boldly."[94] Human life in the flesh is a struggle with the old human and the law, but human life in the spirit is not a struggle; it is the freedom of the faith of Christ.

With the addition of Christ in faith and justification, what had been ethics becomes Christian ethics (or, perhaps more aptly, Christ-in ethics). Works of the law, which were previously actions of a sinner condemned by the law, are now good works, actions of one justified by faith. Christian ethics for Luther, then, is the set of works of the justified sinner, rightly called good works now that they are performed by one whom God holds justified, even though the law condemns him or her. The connection of this Christian ethics to the sacraments is the action of Christ and the Holy Spirit—in short, grace—that unites the Christian with Christ. The Christian receives justification (and sanctification) passively and, as such, is even a passive participant in Christian ethics. This does not mean Luther holds that Christians ought to be passive in the world, but rather Christians are passive before God, and that is exactly the strength of Christian ethics. It is not a passive ethics, but rather an ethics of passivity, through which the presence of Christ becomes real and active in the world.

---

[93] Luther, "Lectures on Galatians, 1535," *LW* 26:35.
[94] Martin Luther, "Letter 91, to Philip Melanchthon, Wartburg, August 1, 1521," *LW* 48:282.

Chapter 3

Sacraments and Ethics in Louis-Marie Chauvet

Introduction

The work of the French Roman Catholic priest Louis-Marie Chauvet has gained considerable popularity and influence recently, particularly in North America.[1] While Chauvet's thought carries implications for a number of areas of theology, this chapter focuses on the connection in his theology between sacraments and ethics.[2] Specifically, this chapter

---

[1] See, for example, the works of Glenn Ambrose and Timothy Brunk already cited, as well as the volume by Philippe Bordeyne and Bruce T. Morrill, eds., *Sacraments: Revelation of the Humanity of God* (Collegeville, MN: Liturgical Press, 2008). See also Joseph C. Mudd, *Eucharist as Meaning: Critical Metaphysics and Contemporary Sacramental Theology* (Collegeville, MN: Liturgical Press, 2014), Todd Townshend, *The Sacramentality of Preaching: Homiletical Uses of Louis-Marie Chauvet's Theology of Sacramentality* (New York: Peter Lang, 2009), Vincent J. Miller, "An Abyss and the Heart of Mediation: Louis-Marie Chauvet's Fundamental Theology of Sacramentality," *Horizons* 24, no. 2 (Fall 1997): 230–47, and Timothy R. Gabrielli, "Chauvet in Space: Louis-Marie Chauvet's Sacramental Account of Christian Identity and the Challenges of a Global Consumer Culture," in *Religion, Economics, and Culture in Conflict and Conversation*, ed. Laurie Cassidy and Maureen H. O'Connell, vol. 56 of the College Theology Society (Maryknoll, NY: Orbis, 2011), 134–56.

[2] For an extended treatment of this topic, see Timothy Brunk, *Liturgy and Life*. This chapter focuses on just those aspects that will bear on the discussion of this subject in relation to Luther.

argues the following: in the thought of Louis-Marie Chauvet, sacraments and ethics are connected by a symbolic exchange between God and humans. This symbolic exchange consists of authentic human reception of God's gifts (grace), which is marked by the action of the human's return-gift as ethics.

In order to develop this thesis, the chapter begins by outlining Chauvet's conception of the symbol and the symbolic. The bulk of Chauvet's theology—particularly his sacramental theology—rests on the foundation of these concepts. For Chauvet, the symbol is not simply one thing that represents another as if it were a placeholder of some kind. The symbol instead bears the presence of that which it symbolizes to the one who receives it, creating a manner of exchange that is wholly alien to market debit and credit. The symbolic order, argues Chauvet, utterly permeates human existence, to the point that language itself belongs to it, at least in part.[3] This first section of the chapter will draw out Chauvet's view of the symbol by exploring how he conceives of language, as well as his move from language to the unavoidability of symbolic mediation in human life. Having sketched these two, the section will finish by arguing that, for Chauvet, the symbolic order is the order within which Christian soteriology and ethics operate.

The second section of the chapter will summarize Chauvet's theological anthropology. If the connection between sacraments and ethics is a symbolic exchange between God and humans, then Chauvet's thought on what or who exactly the human is, as well as how humans relate to God and one another, is an essential component of how Chauvet views that connection. This section will argue that, for Chauvet, the human is essentially an entity that is bodily and relational. Building on his conception of the symbolic order, Chauvet argues that the human experiences reality only as mediated bodily, to the extent that he refers to the human as the "I-body" and the body itself as the "arch-symbol." Additionally, while bodily mediation is the true human situation in Chauvet's thought, this situation requires the human's consent; it is neither self-evident nor easy to grasp in one's experience of life. The bodily mediation of reality also goes beyond the individual human's experience for Chauvet. Not only is the whole of one's experience of reality mediated to one's self bodily, but also one's very self (the I-body)

---

[3] Louis-Marie Chauvet, *The Sacraments: The Word of God at the Mercy of the Body* (Collegeville, MN: Liturgical Press, 1997), 79.

is mediated through what Chauvet calls the "triple body" of culture, tradition, and nature. The human self is, for Chauvet, never a self-contained entity; it is always the result of other persons, communities, and circumstances. The human is irreducibly bodily, and the human is irreducibly relational.

Having highlighted the points of Chauvet's theological anthropology that bear on our discussion of sacraments and ethics, the third section of this chapter will move to describing Chauvet's concept of symbolic exchange. As the center of the entire matter of sacraments and ethics in Chauvet, this concept is crucial both for this chapter and for the conversation with Luther in chapter 4. Symbolic exchange for Chauvet is ultimately the giving and receiving of gifts, outside the realm of market exchange but nevertheless implying action on the parts of both the giver and the receiver. Relying heavily on Marcel Mauss, Chauvet describes symbolic exchange as the giving and receiving not only of goods or services but also of the presence of the giver and receiver within those goods or services. Further, reception of these gifts implies that the receiver will then make a return-gift, not necessarily directly back to the original giver, but forward to other receivers. To receive is to be under the obligation to give. Within this framework, symbolic exchange functions in the Christian tradition through God giving God's own presence to humans in the sacraments, and, in turn, by receiving that gift, humans receive also the obligation to give of themselves to others, to make a return-gift.

The final section of the chapter will bring together the first three sections and move beyond them to a discussion of symbolic efficacy and sacramental grace in Chauvet. The symbolic exchange between God and humans does carry the "requirement" of human action in response to God's gifts, but one ought to ask the question: is this requirement a prerequisite, a marker, or a fruit of the exchange? Further, Chauvet argues that what Christians receive in the symbolic exchange with God in the sacraments is not only God's presence in grace but also their very selves as a task. What humans receive as themselves by the triple body of culture, tradition, and nature is augmented (or even redefined) by their symbolic reception of God in the sacraments. This is the efficacy of sacramental grace in Chauvet—that the human receives her- or himself as a task by grace. In this light, ultimately, the "movement" from sacraments to ethics is something of a misnomer for Chauvet. In Chauvet's view, sacraments and ethics are both intrinsic parts of a symbolic exchange between God and humans, in which humans receive from God both God's self in grace and, by that same gift, also themselves as (ethical) tasks. The chapter will conclude on this point, opening the book to its fourth chapter, in which the theologies of Luther and Chauvet will be drawn into conversation.

1. *The Symbol and the Symbolic*

Louis-Marie Chauvet has articulated a vision of Christianity that revolves around the concept of the symbol and the symbolic. For Chauvet, the symbol is an inextricable component of Christianity, and it is to the symbolic order that the sacraments (and grace) ultimately belong. In order to move toward how Chauvet conceives of the connection between sacraments and ethics, one ought first to understand the order of reality according to which sacraments operate in Chauvet's thought and the modality of which he considers sacraments to be a part. The symbol is the foundation of Chauvet's approach to theology, set over and against what he calls the sign. This chapter explores what Chauvet's concern is in emphasizing the symbol and argues that the symbol is ultimately a mediation of presence (individual and/or corporate), a member of the symbolic order, which is free of instrumentality, value, and empirical calculation.

Problems with Thomas: Causality and Sign

In order to accurately describe what a symbol and the symbolic order are for Chauvet, it would be helpful to delineate what they are *not*; that is, exactly who is Chauvet's dialogue partner as he takes pains to describe the symbolic order, and where does the alternative fall short? By and large, Chauvet presents the symbolic order as an alternative to the way he interprets Thomas Aquinas's theology of grace and the sacraments. According to Chauvet, Thomas's struggles to articulate the sacramental relationship between humans and God ultimately rest on two concepts—causality and sign—both of which Chauvet finds suspect in this regard. In the first place, for Chauvet grace is "a *non*-object, a *non*-value"[4] that is ill-suited for the language of causality. As he argues:

> In Scholastic discourse, the category of *causality* is always tied to the idea of production or augmentation; thus, it always presupposes an explanatory model implying production, sometimes of a technical, sometimes

[4] Chauvet, *Symbol and Sacrament*, 7.

of a biological variety (the germ cell in development), a model in which the idea of "instrumentality" plays a pivotal role. Clearly there is an (apparently fundamental) heterogeneity between the language of grace and the instrumental and productionist language of causality.[5]

Chauvet is careful to point out that while certain Scholastic thinkers incorporated causality into the definition of a sacrament (e.g., Peter Lombard, Duns Scotus, and even the early Thomas), Thomas ultimately resisted doing so in the *Summa Theologiae*.[6] For Thomas, following Augustine, a sacrament is "the sign of a sacred thing," or "the sign of a sacred thing insofar as it sanctifies human beings."[7] Thomas's point, as Chauvet reads him, is that sacraments are in the first place not instruments but representations. They signify what is happening—the giving and receiving of grace—rather than primarily being the cause of that giving and receiving.

Chauvet argues, however, that Thomas returns to causality when he considers what the sacraments *do* in addition to what the sacraments *are*. According to Chauvet, Thomas is concerned to preserve the Scholastic formula that sacraments "effect what they represent,"[8] which requires delving into some kind of causality. Thomas does move away from what Chauvet calls "disposing" causality (the idea that the sacraments contain grace that they then deposit to those who participate in them) but does so only by substituting "instrumental" causality.[9] One might think of the difference between disposing causality and instrumental causality as the difference between a silo and an auger: a silo stores a commodity until it is distributed, while an auger stores nothing but is the mechanism by which the commodity is delivered. To be fair, Chauvet argues that Thomas does not reify grace in quite these stark of terms. As he reads Thomas, grace is an accident rather than a substance, contained in the sacraments only "as a function of a certain instrumental virtue which is something in process and incomplete by nature."[10]

[5] Ibid.

[6] Ibid., 12–15.

[7] Ibid.

[8] Ibid., 17.

[9] Ibid., 16. See also H. F. Dondaine, "A propos d'Avicenne et de S. Thomas: de la causalité dispositive á la causalité instrumentale," *Revue thomiste* 51 (1951): 441–53.

[10] Thomas Aquinas, quoted in Chauvet, *Symbol and Sacrament*, 19.

Nevertheless, Chauvet argues, within Thomas's understanding of the sacraments and grace, "one must say that [the sacraments] effect what they signify. But according to what modality? For Thomas, only one is possible: causality."[11] It is true that Thomas defines sacraments first as belonging to the genus of "sign"[12] and only by way of explanation turns to causality, but Chauvet maintains that the Thomistic understanding of sacramental causality still remains "an ever-present scheme of representation that we call technical or productionist."[13] This technical, productionist, or mechanistic structure of sacraments, Chauvet argues, is alien to the gratuitousness of the Christian concept of grace. Chauvet does not go so far as to maintain that Thomas's sacramental theology is entirely wrong, however. Instead, Chauvet points to what he sees as a necessary element of Thomas's thought that he blames for the perseverance in Thomas of both causality and sign: metaphysics.

For Chauvet (following Guy Lafon), metaphysics unavoidably implies causality because the logic of the metaphysical tradition requires it in order to be thinkable at all. Put another way, indefiniteness, becoming, and movement are all terms that connote transition, impermanence. For metaphysics, says Chauvet, a permanent state of becoming is not possible. What is possible is movement toward some finished "product," or movement *from* some stationary, solid cause. In Chauvet's words,

> Whatever is without limits is, for [metaphysics], beyond thought, defies all logic. The only logic possible is that of a first cause and of an absolute foundation for the totality of existents; that of a center playing the role of a fixed point; that of a presence, faultless, constant, stable.[14]

Within this worldview, causality is inescapable. Any alternative (such as the always-becoming of the symbolic order in which reciprocity never wanes and always develops) is, strictly speaking, unthinkable. This locks Thomas into the logic of causality that, regardless of "every attempt being made to 'purify' this scheme by the use of analogy," ends up reducing grace and the sacraments in Thomas to "the order of value or

---

[11] Chauvet, *Symbol and Sacrament*, 21.

[12] Ibid., 15.

[13] Ibid., 22. For a critique of Chauvet's reading of Thomas, see Mudd, *Eucharist as Meaning*.

[14] Chauvet, *Symbol and Sacrament*, 44.

empirical verifiability."[15] For Chauvet, the debt Thomas's thought owes to metaphysics undermines the essential graciousness and gratuitousness of grace itself.

This problem with the language and logic of causality Chauvet sees extended to the very logic of Thomas's language itself. As Chauvet reads him, Thomas's thought and discourse function according to the logic of sign (as opposed to what Chauvet will call the logic of symbol), in that, for Thomas, language is an instrument used to represent thoughts or analogies; it is a tool used to provide physical, vocal signs for thoughts, which are themselves non-physical. The order of the sign begins with this view of language, namely, that language is a convenient (though not perfect) tool used to catalyze a process whose limiting factor is the efficiency of the tool. It is telling, claims Chauvet, that Thomas seems to share Augustine's opinion that "before [the fall], God perhaps spoke with Adam and Eve in the same way he communicates with the angels, that is, by directly illuminating their intellects with God's permanent truth."[16] Chauvet argues that this "original Platonism," in which the ideal for communication is immediate transfer of truth, and in which linguistic mediation only facilitates the communication process as a necessary evil, is always operative in metaphysics and the thought-systems that rely on it.[17] The main problem with this logic for Chauvet is that "it is impossible, when working under such presuppositions, to develop a positive evaluation for either the body or language as the environment in which both the subject may come to life and truth may happen."[18]

In addition to falling short of affording language, the body, and the subject the credit they deserve, the logic of the sign (Chauvet argues) also is unavoidably subject to the logic of causality, at least insofar as it is used to speak of God. Chauvet points out that for Thomas, while analogy is the primary way to conceive of our language about God, "the validity of our analogies 'is determined by the relation the creature maintains with God as its principle and its cause.'"[19] Built into the operation of language itself concerning the divine is the operation of causality, which brings with it the problems mentioned above. Taken as

---

[15] Ibid., 45.
[16] Ibid., 34–35.
[17] Ibid., 34.
[18] Ibid.
[19] Ibid., 39. Italics removed.

a whole, Chauvet does not maintain that Thomas's approach to sacramental theology is not useful, but he does maintain that Thomas's captivity to the logic of sign and causality impoverishes his theology of grace and the sacraments.

Chauvet's Alternative: The Symbolic

If sign and causality are problematic ways of conceiving of grace and the sacraments, what exactly is the symbolic order that Chauvet suggests as an alternative? Like the order of sign, the symbolic order begins with a view of language and how it works. Instead of a set of tools humans use to describe their world and experiences, however, Chauvet adopts Heidegger's view that "it is language [itself] that speaks."[20] Quoting Heidegger, Chauvet points out that "humans conduct themselves as if they were the masters of language, while in fact it is language that governs them."[21] Chauvet means to emphasize the idea that language constructs reality and experience as much as it describes it. Nevertheless, one ought to note here that Chauvet's final goal in affording language such primacy is to emphasize the embodied nature of humanity, not to emphasize the power of language simply for its own sake.[22] While language certainly contains a "pole" of utility,[23] that is, a pole associated with describing things and experiences for those who use it, this pole of language for Chauvet is contained within a "second, more fundamental pole."[24] This second pole of language is, for Chauvet, the more essential pole and is the pole that he associates with the symbolic order.

This more fundamental pole of language may be called the pole of linguistic "summons." As language builds reality, it does so by *summoning* it, calling it into being and making it so. Accordingly, when something (or someone) enters reality, such an event is a language-event, an event of speech. Even further, spoken words are only one aspect of this pole of language, because this pole of language extends to silence and listening. Humans are always speaking, simply by living. Human experience and life is made possible, summoned, by the operation of lan-

---

[20] Martin Heidegger, quoted in ibid., 55.

[21] Chauvet, *Symbol and Sacrament*, 55.

[22] In this, Chauvet departs from Heidegger. Chauvet is interested in the body; for all intents and purposes, it seems Heidegger is interested in being, language, and ultimately the poetic.

[23] Chauvet, *Symbol and Sacrament*, 106–7.

[24] Ibid., 56.

guage. Language does not stand outside reality or cover it like a coat of paint. Language is the very foundation, studs, and rafters of humans' experience of reality itself (though it is the embodied human community that has by its action of living instituted those foundations, studs, and rafters). For Chauvet, the pole of language that summons—that is, language considered symbolically—*makes* human reality.

Language also goes beyond summoning human experience to humans; it is similarly a *mediation*.[25] A mediation of what? For Chauvet, language mediates reality to the subjects who receive it. It builds reality and also mediates it to its participants. Language goes beyond being an instrument that stands beside and outside its content as a sign; it is a process and body that participates in, shapes, and creates reality for those who use it.[26] In this way language, operative according to the logic of the symbol, is something shared between those who use it, and its content and meaning are furthermore subject to understanding between those who use it. Symbolic language is a mediator of reality between subjects and is therefore also a mediator of identity.

The characteristics and makeup of human identity in Chauvet's thought occupy the second section of this chapter, but the mediatory nature of symbolic language provides a useful bridge from discussing the symbolic as language to speaking of the symbolic itself. Symbolic language is inseparable from the systems of meaning (or bodies of reality) of which it is a part. Likewise for Chauvet, human subjects are only possible because of their relations to other human subjects,[27] that is, because of their participation in a preexistent cultural milieu. Both symbolic language and the subject can function only as parts of a larger body, system, or agreement of understanding between participants, because both are at their base actions of participation. In Chauvet's words, "subject and language build themselves up in tandem."[28] Symbolic language mediates identity because it is the *via* of subjects relating to one another. Beyond simply relating one subject's ideas and thoughts to another subject, language as symbolic bears with it the one subject to the other. It is more than ideas that are exchanged; the subjects themselves share each other with one another.

[25] Ibid., 87.
[26] Ibid., 89.
[27] Ibid., 95.
[28] Ibid., 86.

As an example, imagine an international student coming to the United States from France, a student whose English-speaking skills are passible but strained by this new challenge. Imagine that on the first or second day of classes, as this student is navigating his or her way around the bustling college campus (swimming in a language quite different from the student's native French), the student encounters two other students who are sitting on a bench conversing with each other in French, discussing their favorite local coffee shops. Further, these two students do not just converse in French but do so making use of all the idioms, inflections, and nuances that a native French-speaker would use in describing his or her favored coffee places. Two things immediately happen for the international student, one on the level of sign and the other on the level of symbol. First, the student is able to understand what the French-speaking pair is saying, allowing the student to eavesdrop or ignore the conversation at will, perhaps gathering information on the best places to grab a morning cup. *This* is the level of sign.

Beyond this utility, however (and beyond the student's interest or lack thereof in the subject of coffee shops), the student recognizes two concrete other students who can share a conversation in French, opening up the possibility of engaging them in conversation and perhaps even getting acquainted. Language moves beyond content to the possibility of action and participation. Regardless of whether the student actually approaches this conversing pair, the student's world has been changed (either slightly or not-so-slightly), because the action of the pair conversing in French has been *shared* by the exchange student. *This* is the level of symbol: the international student does not simply come away from the encounter with some information about coffee houses; he or she comes away with the knowledge and experience that there are others close at hand who can share and understand a familiar system of meaning. The conversing pair of subjects has not simply shared their thoughts on coffee; the pair has also, at some basic level at least, shared *themselves*.

If this is concretely what the symbolic might look like, what can we actually say about the symbolic order itself? If the symbolic itself connotes an "order" (and it does in Chauvet's thought), it does not do so as an operation of language distinct from but nevertheless equivalent to the order of the sign. It operates only as embodied in a context (something of which the sign is independent, since the sign represents rather than mediates reality). A symbol without the content of a context is an empty symbol, which for Chauvet is no symbol at all. The logic of the symbol cannot function without participating in a *specific, embodied* symbolic order. In Chauvet's words, "It is the entire symbolic order to which it belongs . . . that a symbol evokes."[29] This is why language, for all its power in constructing reality, depends also on the participation of embodied communities and contexts for its own reality. As Chauvet describes it, language has both an *instituting* and *instituted* character.[30]

Language (and the symbol) is both instituted and instituting because it is ultimately bound to its operation between subjects and within embodied communities. For our student above, the use of his or her native French brought that system of meaning and all its content suddenly to bear on a context in which the student did not expect it. It was not simply the French words that were significant but also what they carried with them; they revealed the presence of those who shared the system of symbols connoted by the use of the French language. The symbol is a shared reality, built up as a common possession and frame of reference, whose utility is "not primarily a function of *representation* of objects, but of *communication* between subjects."[31] As such, the symbol operates as "a mediation for mutual recognition between subjects and for their identification within their world."[32] The symbol does not signify; it embodies. It does not represent; it mediates. While the sign points to an entity or thing, the symbol bears that entity or thing within itself as a presence communicated to its participants. The sign is a tool; the symbol is an action.

The importance of recognizing the symbol as an action between subjects is that it locates the makeup of reality within the communal action/sharing of the subjects who experience that reality, rather than in the reality itself, which the subjects would describe from without. Chauvet then moves on to speak of the sacraments—and grace operative therein—as symbolic actions in this sense, building a reality that they then bear to their participants. (This is explained further in sections 2 and 3 below.) Recognition of the symbolic order does not, however, happen spontaneously; Chauvet insists it requires a consent, namely, a consent by the subject to what he calls the "presence of an absence."[33] If, within the symbolic order, reality is mediated to subjects who

---

[29] Ibid., 115.
[30] Ibid., 377.
[31] Ibid., 121.
[32] Ibid., 116. Italics removed.
[33] Ibid., 98–99.

participate in it, then there is some separation, some breach, between the subject and the reality he or she experiences. Immediacy is not possible, even to one's self. This absence that is present, of subjects to their reality, subjects to each other, and even subjects to themselves, is a necessary limitation of human existence for Chauvet, because human existence is conditioned by the symbolic (i.e., the shared building up of context, reality, and even subjects themselves). Such truth requires recognition first and then consent by the subject, because we humans often live our lives as if this absence were not part of our reality. Consenting to the presence of this absence is not humans' "default" view.

Before losing the discussion's focus on the symbol by working endlessly to describe the symbolic and consent to symbolic mediation, one ought to recognize that to speak of the symbol in the abstract is a doomed exercise from the start, as the symbolic exists only as concrete symbols in concrete symbolic orders. We have listed some characteristics of the symbol, but we also must put off a full exploration of the symbolic until this discussion turns specifically to the context within which Chauvet develops his thought on the symbol: the Christian context of Scripture, sacraments, and ethics. In order to do so, this chapter now turns to Chauvet's theological anthropology, in order to lay the groundwork for his theology of sacraments and ethics.

2. *Theological Anthropology*

Two concepts dominate Chauvet's theological anthropology: the truth of the bodily mediation of reality and the intrinsic communality of human identity. For Chauvet, just as language belongs (at least in part) to the symbolic order, so are humans' experiences of reality mediated to and through them by the symbolic order. The vehicle for this mediation is the body in all of its aspects—speech, the senses, and the mind's faculties—but while language for Chauvet operates on the level of both symbol and sign, in truth the human can only apprehend reality symbolically, that is, bodily. Further, the bodily mediation of reality extends beyond the individual human body. As Chauvet conceives of the body, it includes the corporate aspects and influences of one's culture (meaning, for Chauvet, one's social location), the tradition of which one is a part (specifically, for Chauvet, one's family tradition), and nature (one's interaction with the environment and cosmos). These "bodies" constitute the human self as much as a human's own body does, and this intrinsic relationality of the human person, this dependence for one's identity on factors that are outside one's control or influence, means for the human that not only is reality bodily mediated but the truth of that mediation in its fullness also requires the human's consent. Speaking ecclesially (since the goal in this chapter is to move toward the "theological" portion of Chauvet's theological anthropology), this means ultimate reality—God—can in truth only be experienced symbolically, that is, mediated through bodies: physical, cultural, traditional, and natural.

Chauvet's view of the human person develops from the same set of insights that informs his view of language and symbol, the foremost of which is a suspicion of immediacy. Just as language for Chauvet does not function as pure instrument or sign (i.e., language does not give the human who "uses" it an immediate experience of reality), neither does the human person experience any aspect of reality—even one's own self—as immediate. Unlike language, however, which Chauvet argues is always partially made up of symbol and sign,[34] the human self and experience of reality is utterly symbolic, that is, never immediate. This is not to say that humans never *believe* they experience themselves and reality without mediation, however. Contrarily, what Chauvet calls the "temptation of immediacy"[35] is an ever-present part of human life (and is also a temptation that can play out ecclesially, as we will discuss below).

If immediacy is a temptation and ultimately impossible, exactly what sort of mediation characterizes human existence and selfhood? What symbol or set of symbols bear reality to the human person, and bear the human person to her- or himself? In Chauvet's view, this is the role of the body and corporeality. Humans inhabit a physical world and are made up of matter. This means for Chauvet that the entirety of human existence is physical and subject to corporeal mediation to the human, who is also irreducibly physical. Further, the human body is not a neutral instrument of reception, as if its sole purpose were to mediate the external world to some interior, ethereal self. The very concept that there is some interior self is erroneous for Chauvet; quoting Nietzsche, Chauvet claims, " 'Body am I, entirely and completely, and nothing besides.' This saying by Nietzsche is to be taken literally."[36] Chauvet's point is that

---

[34] Chauvet, *The Sacraments*, 79.

[35] Ibid., 39.

[36] Chauvet, *Symbol and Sacrament*, 149. At this point, I have my own reservations with regard to Chauvet's theological anthropology. The idea that the body mediates

any view of the human that seeks to preserve some nonphysical aspect of humanity (read: the disembodied "soul") misses the mark entirely. The human is *always* bodily, in every way. Every aspect of the human is mediated corporeally, both to one's self and to others. On this basis, Chauvet prefers to speak of the human person as an "I-body": "What kind of thing is the I-body? Necessarily *my own body*, irreducible to any other, and yet, in the midst of its difference, recognizing itself to be similar to every other I-body."[37] The I-body is Chauvet's fundamental anthropological construct. For him, the body is what ultimately differentiates one human from another, so it acts as something like the border of selfhood. Others know this or that human by his or her *being* this or that body, and a human knows her- or himself as distinct from others most essentially by recognizing the borders of one's own body.[38] The human "I" experiences reality—receives reality, including the self—by means of the body.

The body is also more than a neutral instrument of reception in that it expresses human reality in addition to mediating it. In Chauvet's view, the human as I-body speaks selfhood bodily. Again, this does not mean that Chauvet believes there is an entity "inside" the human body that simply expresses itself through the human body; rather, who the human *is* is both expressed and created bodily. For Chauvet, the body is in this sense "speech."[39] As language symbolically builds reality, so does the body build the reality of the human. As (symbolic) language bears the presence of the speaker to the hearer, so does the body bear the presence of the human to the world surrounding her or him. The body as speech

---

reality suggests to me that there ought to be some entity *to whom* reality is being mediated. This quotation of Nietzsche only exacerbates the problem, because my objection is based exactly on the idea that Christianity (to my reading) claims that there *is* some element of the human that is "beyond" the body in some sense. I do not mean to claim that there is some human entity that is *separate from* the body but rather that Chauvet's emphasis on the bodily mediation of reality ends up reducing human existence to physicality. Taken to its extreme (something against which Chauvet does not guard), this implies something close to biological determinism: we humans are ultimately wonderfully constructed machines, the only mystery of which consists in the incompleteness of our understanding of how these machines (humans) work. Such an implication, I believe, is incompatible with the Christian tradition.

[37] Chauvet, *Symbol and Sacrament*, 149.
[38] Ibid.
[39] Ibid., 146.

means for Chauvet that "humans do not ex-sist except as corporality whose concrete place is always their own bodies."[40] The body is not merely instrumental for the human; it is symbolic. It both mediates reality and creates it and does so as the most basic and essential mode of human experience. The body is, for Chauvet, the arch-symbol.[41]

Like the raw concept of the symbol, the corporeal, symbolic mediation of reality and human identity is inseparable from its context. The human I-body does not exist on his or her own as a monad separate from his or her temporal and historical surroundings; in fact, the body as speech implies for Chauvet not the body's *own* speech but that the I-body lives as "spoken" by his or her context: "This unique body is 'speaking' only because it is already spoken by a culture, because it is the recipient of a tradition, and is tightly bonded with a world."[42] For Chauvet, the I-body *is* only the I-body because it depends on external, corporate bodies for its own existence and identity. Specifically, Chauvet names three corporate bodies responsible for speaking the identity of a human. First, the body of culture of which the I-body is a part provides a "system of values or symbolic network" that gives texture to the existence of the I-body.[43] The cultural body supplies the language of the I-body (which, as we have discussed, is more than instrumental words; cultural language creates the everyday context of which the I-body is a part). It gives the I-body his or her experience of the world while also providing the very linguistic conditions for appropriating that experience.

Second, the I-body is also spoken by a body of tradition, which for Chauvet consists of something like the cultural body, but extended back into history. While one might think of the cultural body as the current set of circumstances in which (and because of which) the I-body lives, the body of tradition represents the historical conditions, narratives, and events that, taken as a set, have led to that current set of circumstances. The body of tradition is for Chauvet one "whose foundation is always more or less mythic and of which [the I-body] is, often unconsciously, a kind of living memory."[44]

---

[40] Ibid., 146.
[41] Ibid., 151.
[42] Ibid., 149–50.
[43] Ibid., 150.
[44] Ibid.

The third external body—that of nature—is for Chauvet the cosmic body, the universe, anthropomorphized such that it provides the human I-body a permanent, natural dialogue partner.[45] On one level this means for Chauvet that the body of nature is the part of the I-body's environment that is not ultimately formed by other humans, but beyond this Chauvet means by the body of nature to connote the source of what might be called "natural symbols": "the alternations of day and night, the cycle of the seasons, and . . . the fundamental oppositions of earth-sky, water-fire, mountains-abysses, light-shadow, and so forth."[46] These natural symbols provide something of a common human experience or symbolic framework, at least to the extent that they are phenomena available to all humans.

Chauvet does not imply that these three bodies (culture, tradition, and nature) are in any way separate from one another; they are for him three interwoven aspects that, while remaining larger than and logically prior to the I-body, nevertheless together constitute the I-body as an entity.[47] The body as arch-symbol requires a context in order to function symbolically, and that is what the triple body provides. The human, then, is bodily mediated and constituted both in the sense that the I-body is always subject to physicality and in the sense that the bodies of culture, tradition, and nature speak through that physicality as a

---

[45] Ibid.

[46] Ibid.

[47] This is another point at which I have reservations concerning Chauvet's theological anthropology. If the I-body exists only as "spoken" by the triple body of culture, tradition, and nature, then there is precious little room for uniqueness and mystery in personhood. For Chauvet (to my reading at least), every part of the I-body depends in some respect on some part or parts of the triple body that precedes it. This precipitates a human person who is *only* the sum of his or her parts and whose uniqueness is contingent upon the uniqueness of his or her historical, cultural, and natural attributes. Compare this with, for example, the theological anthropology of John Zizioulas, in which one's personhood is still constituted in relation to others and the natural world but also in which the uniqueness of the person consists precisely in the ineffability of the person. See, for example, John Zizioulas, *Being as Communion* (Crestwood, NY: Saint Vladimir's Seminary, 2002), esp. chap. 1; also John Zizioulas, *Communion and Otherness* (London: T&T Clark, 2006), esp. chap. 2. In Zizioulas, the person at his or her foundation is uniqueness and mystery; for Chauvet, the person at his or her foundation is the speech of the triple body. In essence for Chauvet, without nuance (which Chauvet does not, to my reading, provide), the I-body—the person—is ultimately a consequence, not an agent.

corporate (or one might say relational) constitution of the person. In Chauvet's words, "Each one of us is what he or she is only to the extent that each one 'retains' in one's self and 'extends' to others this triple body of which each is, as it were, a living memory."[48] This concept certainly contains tensions, but we will attend to these more fully in chapter 4.

Thus far this section has outlined the specifically anthropological vision of Chauvet's theological anthropology. Chauvet constructs this view of the human person always with an eye to its theological implications, however, specifically its implications for the life of the church as the locus of bodily mediation (that is to say, the true, symbolic experience) of divine reality. This ecclesial dimension of Chauvet's thought, like his thought on the symbolic order of language and the body, is not immune to the temptation of immediacy. There is a strong allure to the idea that we humans in some way can "directly" experience God, and this idea can often be reinforced by overzealous or mistaken interpretations of religious encounters and practices, particularly the sacraments. As Chauvet points out,

> In their significant materiality, the sacraments thus constitute an un-avoidable stumbling block which forms a barrier to every imaginary claim to a direct connection, individual and interior, with Christ or to a Gnostic-like, illuminist contact with him. They represent the indefeasible mediations, beginning with the Church, outside of which there is no possible Christian faith. They tell us that the faith has a body, that it adheres to our body. More than that, they tell us that to become a believer is to learn to consent, without resentment, to the corporality of the faith.[49]

This consent is an essential aspect of Christianity for Chauvet. Like the fundamental constitution of the human, the fundamental constitution of the Christian is symbolic mediation, that is, bodily mediation both in the sense of the human I-body and in the sense of the corporate ecclesial body. The role of the "individual" human I-body (to the extent that such an entity is present in Chauvet's thought) is to consent to the truth of this mediation.

[48] Chauvet, *Symbol and Sacrament*, 150.
[49] Ibid., 153.

One can view such consent in Chauvet as roughly under two forms: first, the consent to Christianity as subject to mediation through the physicality of sacraments and the historicity of culture and tradition and, second, the consent to Christianity as subject to the mediation of the body of Christians together, that is, the church. The first form of consent springs naturally from Chauvet's thought on symbol and the body—since there is no nonphysical aspect of the human, divine presence can only come *to* the human *in* concrete historical circumstances and *through* concrete embodied practices. This is not a limitation of the power of God in Chauvet's eyes but rather a fact springing from the very mode of human existence God created in the first place. The temptation to conceive of God and Christian faith as somehow outside the symbolic order or not subject to bodily mediation is ever-present to the Christian, but true Christian faith for Chauvet nevertheless consents to a space between the human and the divine, a void across which the divine travels in order to reach humans, or in a phrase Chauvet uses, a "presence of an absence."[50]

The second form of consent—the consent of the Christian to the necessary mediation of the church—represents the ecclesial reflection in Chauvet of the priority of the triple body in constituting the identity of the I-body. In this conception, just as the triple body of culture, tradition, and nature is prior to and constitutive of the I-body, so is the body of the church prior to and constitutive of the Christian. In Chauvet's words, "It is not that women and men, in some way attached directly to Jesus Christ, would be Christians separately and by banding together would form the church. In order to be Christian, one must belong to the church. The church is primary."[51] That Christians may think of themselves as gathering together to form the church is not surprising for Chauvet, but ultimately such a view is illusory. The church (with its traditions, practices, Scriptures, and systems of morality) provides Christians the symbolic context required to even conceive of the name "Christian." The content of that label is inextricable from the communal, ecclesial context that gave it birth.

This section has argued that Chauvet's theological anthropology is founded on the twin core themes of bodily/symbolic mediation and

---

[50] Ibid., 177. This term will require further discussion below, as it both implies the inescapability of bodily mediation and also departure of Jesus and yet presence thereby (this second aspect is discussed in section 4 of this chapter below).

[51] Chauvet, *The Sacraments*, 31.

communality. Human truth, for Chauvet, is that the human I-body is constituted symbolically by the triple body of culture, tradition, and nature. The triple body speaks the I-body into existence by providing both its context and content. In the Christian tradition, the church represents the triple body in this sense: that it is prior to individual Christian identity. The church provides the symbolic context that gives life and meaning to Christian Scriptures, sacraments, and actions.[52] To be a human for Chauvet is to be intrinsically connected to (spoken by) one's social, historical, and natural context. To be a Christian for Chauvet is to be intrinsically connected to (spoken by) the church, its traditions, and its practices. Having articulated this, the discussion can now move to the specific connection between symbolic exchange and the sacraments in Chauvet and is poised to attend to some anthropological tensions in Chauvet in the fourth chapter below.

3. Symbolic Exchange and the Sacraments

For Chauvet, the sacraments are essentially practices of symbolic exchange between humans and God. As the term suggests, symbolic exchange is giving and receiving according to the symbolic order. What exactly that looks like, what its characteristics are, and what implications are intrinsic to the concept constitute the bulk of this section. To begin, this section explores symbolic exchange as Chauvet's view of the gift, implying its immunity to value, calculation, and instrumentality, as well as its requirement of a response, specifically a "return-gift." This concept of symbolic exchange Chauvet uses as a way to then discuss grace, which is the second subject of this section. Specifically, Chauvet views grace not as an object to be exchanged or some kind of "stuff" that one can receive but rather as a reception of oneself. This self-reception Chauvet also calls a "symbolic labor," a telling term that will be useful for dialogue with Luther. Finally, this section locates symbolic exchange and grace in the context Chauvet places them: the liturgical assembly and the sacraments. For Chauvet, the sacraments are fundamentally actions of the celebrating community, *as* actions of that community. The liturgical assembly is for Chauvet a "complex moral person" and a "womb" wherein Christian selves are formed and born. On the basis of this

---

[52] We will return to this triad in section 4, as these three together constitute Chauvet's fullest view of Christianity.

discussion, the chapter will then be able to progress into its fourth section, specifically on the connection in Chauvet between sacraments and ethics.

Symbolic Exchange: The Gift

At the outset one ought to recognize that Chauvet constructs the concept of symbolic exchange with the goal of using it as a model for speaking about grace: "The outstanding characteristic of [symbolic exchange] is that it functions *outside the order of value*. Because of this, it opens for us a possible path by which to theologically conceive of this 'marvelous exchange' (*admirabile commercium*) between God and humankind which we call *grace*."[53] In this light, Chauvet's project is from the beginning a theological project rather than a philosophical or phenomenological one. Chauvet bases his idea of symbolic exchange largely on the observations of Marcel Mauss concerning the concept of the gift (as well as the discussions springing from Mauss's seminal work, *Essai sur le don*), but his goal is to use Mauss's observations as the skeleton for a theology of gift giving.

The first major point that Chauvet draws from Mauss is that within human communities there exists a certain logic of exchange that is separate from the logic of debit and credit that constitutes market exchange. This immunity to what Chauvet calls the order of value (the order of market exchange) is one of two main defining characteristics of symbolic exchange as opposed to all other kinds of transfer of goods and services. According to this logic of non-value, the "stuff" that travels from giver to receiver does not contain its own value, specifically its own utilitarian value.[54] The fact that the stuff may in fact be useful and even indispensable to the receiver (e.g., food, hospitality, clothing) remains foreign to the logic of non-value. What *is* important is the exchange itself, because as Chauvet articulates, "The true objects being exchanged are the subjects themselves."[55]

While the logic of non-value does not allow for calculation of monetary debit and credit, according to Chauvet (and Mauss) it does include obligations and requirements. This is the second main defining characteristic of symbolic exchange, what Chauvet calls "obligatory

---

[53] Chauvet, *Symbol and Sacrament*, 100. Emphasis in original.
[54] Ibid., 101.
[55] Ibid., 106.

generosity."[56] To begin, while the exchange of goods and services may not be required because of its *monetary utility* according to the logic of non-value, it *is* required because of its social significance. Generosity— that is, giving according to the logic of non-value—is required because its absence constitutes the tearing of social fabric. As Chauvet points out, "One gives *without counting*, but this 'gift' is *obligatory*, for 'to refuse to give would be equivalent to declaring war, that is, to refusing alliance and communion.'"[57] This runs counter to what we humans generally think of as the gift: something given without thought or care for recip- rocation. Nevertheless, this oxymoronic nature of symbolic exchange is what allows it to function at all for Chauvet (similar to the way Mauss treats the gift in his work).

Conversely, the reason *to* show generosity in keeping with symbolic exchange is not simply to avoid the consequences of social turmoil. If this were the case, one easily slips into attempting to calculate "how much" generosity is needed in order to keep things running smoothly, or "how often" one ought to be generous in order to stay in good stand- ing with one's neighbors. Such questions are antithetical to the logic of symbolic exchange and non-value, because "how much is required?" and "how often ought I?" are essentially *based* on the calculation of value. These questions are only valid if one is counting the cost of generosity, which is for Chauvet a contradiction in terms. The principle of cost is foreign to the logic of symbolic exchange; instead, "the principle which rules here is one of *super-abundance*."[58]

The principle of super-abundance captures the positive motivating factor for obligatory generosity. The initiation of symbolic exchange has more to do with the abundance of the giver than it does the want or need of the receiver. This results, again, from the fact that what is given and received in symbolic exchange is more than the stuff that is trans- ferred. What is given and received is the giver her- or himself, which implies that the very constitution of one's identity is tied directly (within symbolic exchange) to one's generosity. To the extent that one extends generosity, one is a member of the community and a full, active subject. Identity is integrally bound up with generosity. In Chauvet's words,

---

[56] Ibid., 101–2.
[57] Ibid.,102. Emphasis in original.
[58] Ibid., 106. Emphasis in original.

By the intermediary of these objects [of symbolic exchange], the subjects weave or reweave *alliances*, they *recognize* themselves as full members of the tribe, where they find their *identity* in showing themselves in their proper place, and in putting others in their "proper place." As a consequence, what is transpiring in symbolic exchange is of the same order as what is transpiring in language. . . . In both cases, it is a matter of reversible recognition of each other as fully a *subject*.[59]

The "reversible" nature of recognition in symbolic exchange that Chauvet mentions here means that obligatory generosity does not end with the initial giver. The recipients of said generosity also incur obligation by *being* the recipients. When one person or group receives anything from another, that person or group then comes under the obligation to "return" generosity. One ought not to read this "return" as reciprocity, however. The return of generosity does not flow straight back from the receiver to the giver in a flat reversal of roles. Rather, the return of generosity one can only loosely call a return, because it flows from the receiver *to some third party*, and from that third party to yet another, and another beyond that, constituting a circle of generosity—or, better, a web of generosity—rather than a one-dimensional call-and-response. Strictly speaking, then, the initial giver in symbolic exchange is never *only* a giver, because he or she has also received and will likely receive again, and the initial receiver is never *only* a receiver, because he or she will give in the future and has likely already been a giver. Again, calculation of value does not enter this web of generosity; in fact, it *cannot* without undoing the very basis of the web. Every giver gives because giving is what constitutes identity, and every giver *can* give because he or she is also a receiver. Likewise, every receiver receives because receiving recognizes others as subjects and members of the community, and every receiver *can* receive as a member of the community because he or she has also *given*.

Symbolic Exchange: Grace

At this point we can return to Chauvet's initial goal: using symbolic exchange as a model for speaking theologically about grace. The two main defining characteristics of symbolic exchange (the logic of non-value and obligatory generosity) Chauvet translates roughly theologically into the terms "graciousness" and "gratuitousness," on the one hand,

---

[59] Ibid., 106–7. Emphasis in original.

and "symbolic labor," on the other. Graciousness—at least the way in which Chauvet defines the term—connotes the immunity of God's gifts to value judgments and calculation. This is hardly anything new or earth shattering; few theologians would maintain that by grace we enter a market exchange with our Creator. What the model of symbolic exchange does provide for Chauvet in terms of graciousness, however, is the additional point that what God gives in grace is not external to God's self and us human subjects but actually *is* God's self and we human subjects. This insight in itself is also hardly novel, but the model of symbolic exchange casts this insight under a slightly different light in two ways. First, symbolic exchange implies that whatever we receive from God— that is, everything, from our possessions to our very lives—can be a bearer of God's life and presence to us. Privileged places for this symbolic exchange are, of course, the sacraments, where the Christian tradition claims without reservation that God gives God's self to humans.

Second, because all that humans have is ultimately a gift from God, humankind is constituted from the very beginning as a receiver of gifts, which writes into our very humanity the logic of non-value. This second point is what Chauvet calls gratuitousness: the dependence of humans for the entirety of their reality on their reception of God's freely given gifts (which are of the order of non-value).[60] Furthermore, humans' status as receivers means that every human also receives her- or him*self* in this way. A person is not an autonomous entity; a person is a recipient of all that constitutes him or her. To echo our earlier discussion, the person receives the triple body of culture, tradition, and nature and, through this reception (because symbolic exchange bears the giver in the gift), also receives in some way the One who created the triple body. Likewise in the sacraments, God as the initiator of the symbolic exchange sets humans first as receivers of God's self and thereby also receivers of *them*selves. The graciousness and gratuitousness of symbolic exchange with God means that humans, who receive both God and themselves in this exchange, are constituted in the logic of non-value.

In addition to graciousness and gratuitousness, human self-reception in a symbolic exchange with God (that is, grace) implies a response from the receiver like any other symbolic exchange. In Chauvet's words,

[60] Chauvet, *Symbol and Sacrament*, 108.

Every gift obligates; there is no reception of anything *as a gift* which does not require some return-gift. . . . By the very structure of the exchange, the gratuitousness of the gift *carries the obligation of the return-gift of a response.* Therefore, theologically, grace requires not only this initial gratuitousness on which everything else depends but also the *graciousness of the whole circuit,* and especially of the return-gift. This graciousness qualifies the return-gift as beyond-price, without calculation—in short, as a response of love. *Even the return-gift of our human response thus belongs to the theologically Christian concept of "grace."*[61]

This quote contains a number of elements, but Chauvet's central point is a reemphasis of obligatory generosity in symbolic exchange. The gifts of God to humans are really free, but within their reception is contained the obligation to carry those gifts forward, to "re-gift" in a way. This results not from a string attached to the gift[62] but from the logic according to which gift giving and symbolic exchange operate. To receive a gift—in this case to receive grace—and, on the other hand, to attempt to *not* respond, or to respond according to the logic of value and market exchange ("God has given me x, which is worth y, so I am obligated to respond with z works of charity"), misses the point of symbolic exchange.

Reception of grace in symbolic exchange according to Chauvet is completed by (and thus ultimately depends on) the human response of love.[63] Love, like grace, hoewever, is not quantifiable or subject to value calculation. It can only be exchanged symbolically—that is, as a gift—which means that while reception of grace (which, as we said above, is also human self-reception; humans receive themselves in grace) requires human action to be complete, that human action is not measurable according to any system of value and calculation. The symbolic exchange with God that is grace includes what Chauvet calls "symbolic labor," that is, human labor or work that, like symbolic exchange, operates according to the logic of non-value.[64] Labor that is not subject to calculation runs counter to most of the ways in which Western societies conceive of labor, but essentially it is Chauvet's way of explaining that

---

[61] Ibid., 108–9. Emphasis in original.

[62] At least, Chauvet does not see humans' obligatory response in this way. Whether or not this actually *does* proclaim grace with "strings attached" is a question we will explore further in chapter 4.

[63] Chauvet, *Symbol and Sacrament,* 109.

[64] Ibid., 109, 442.

the obligatory human response of love to the symbolic exchange of grace ought to encompass the whole of human life. In grace, the human receives her- or himself, but receives her- or himself as a task.

The reception of oneself as a task is the point at which Chauvet's view of the human person and his theology of sacraments and grace intertwine. The sacraments are loci of grace, but like every other aspect of human existence, grace does not enter human life without mediation. If grace is the gift of the human self as a task *for* the human self, then the sacraments are the mediations through which that symbolic exchange takes place. As Chauvet articulates, "A sacrament is an 'event of grace' not because it is a field in which a treasure is buried but because it symbolically ploughs the field that we ourselves are and thus renders it fruitful by converting it to . . . *filiation* and *brotherly and sisterly love*."[65] By his comments in this vein Chauvet means to make the point that while the sacraments are mediations of symbolic exchange with God, the sacramental grace operative therein—while it begins in the context of the church—extends to the whole of Christian life in the world, that is, ethics. What takes place in the specifically ecclesial context impacts and even defines Christian living in the world; symbolic exchange in church translates into symbolic labor everywhere: the "affirmation of 'sacramental grace' is simply the concrete unfolding of the general affirmation of the world as the eschatological place of God."[66]

While the sacraments mediate the symbolic exchange that moves the human to symbolic labor, the location of the sacraments as actions of the church is not accidental for Chauvet. His concept of symbolic exchange connects action in the context of the church to action beyond the church, but the church itself is nevertheless essential for this connection. For Chauvet, the church exists as part of the triple body that constitutes the human person, and, as such, it forms Christian identity in the same way as do other aspects of human identity that are given to the person rather than made by the person. The church is a context, an institution and body of symbols in which the symbolic exchange called grace can coherently take place. That is, the church is the body wherein God's action of grace can be named and recognized for what it is.

Chauvet's insistence on the necessity of the ecclesial body (for the mediation of symbolic exchange/grace) does not imply a retreat in his

---

[65] Ibid., 442.
[66] Ibid., 537. Italics removed.

thinking to an *extra ecclesiam nulla salus* soteriology. The necessity of mediation by the church is about Christian identity for Chauvet, not about salvation.[67] Chauvet specifically addresses this question when he states that his model of Christian identity "does not mean 'outside the Church, there is no salvation,' but rather, 'outside the Church, there is no *recognized* salvation.' "[68] Whatever the implications of this remark are for soteriology, it is essential for understanding what Chauvet claims about the role of the church in Christian identity. Recognition of the church and its mediatory role—that is, comprehension of the ecclesial symbolic world, followed by consent to mediation of the divine by that body of meaning and reality—is what makes the symbolic exchange of grace particularly Christian. Chauvet does not claim that grace does not exist or cannot operate outside the church. Rather, to speak of grace and its operation for Chauvet intrinsically evokes the entire symbolic body of meaning and reality that the church constitutes. To recognize grace and salvation is already to use language that has meaning only in the context of the body for whom those terms are formative, that is, the church (or, at the very least, to speak of grace and salvation "without" the church robs the terms of a measure of their richness and content).

For Chauvet, the church (and more specifically the liturgical assembly) is also more than just the context of Christian identity. It is *indispensable for* Christian identity, to the point that Chauvet can claim, "It is not that women and men, in some way attached directly to Jesus Christ, would be Christians separately and by banding together would form the church. In order to be Christian, one must belong to the church."[69] That is, in Chauvet's thought, there is no such thing as an individual Christian, except by the fact that such a person exists within the church. This is one piece of the ecclesial import of mediation, but there is another: the liturgical assembly, as a corporate body, also exhibits its own agency. For Chauvet, just as the church is not a conglomeration of individual Christians, so is the church's action not just a conglomeration of individual Christian wills. This is most apparent with regard to the liturgical assembly, in that the sacraments are never the actions of only one or a few but of the entire liturgical community. The church in the sacraments acts as one, not because Christians will the same thing alongside one

---

[67] One might rightly ask whether Chauvet can adequately address one without implying the other, but for the purposes of the current discussion, we will allow his distinction to stand.

[68] Chauvet, *Symbol and Sacrament*, 180.

[69] Chauvet, *The Sacraments*, 31.

another, but because by their consent to the mediation of the church, the church's action forms their actions (just as the church's identity forms Christians' identities). Further, while this corporate agency of the church begins in a specifically liturgical context, it also extends beyond the liturgical assembly. What is formed as a common liturgical action grows out into common ethical action, making the liturgical assembly what Chauvet calls a "complex moral person."[70] Such a creation, as well as how Chauvet sees this complex moral agency at work in Christian ethical life, is the subject of this chapter's fourth section below. Beginning with an outline of Chauvet's tri-pole model of the church, the fourth section returns to the issues of consent, corporate agency, and how these inform symbolic efficacy and sacramental grace (that is, how they facilitate the connection of sacraments and ethics).

4. Sacraments and Ethics

Sacraments and ethics in Chauvet are connected ultimately as two-thirds of a three-pronged model of the Christian community, the church. Along with scripture, sacraments and ethics comprise the context in which Christians are formed as such, that is, the context in which and through which Christians receive their identity as Christians by grace. Given the above discussions of symbolic exchange, the makeup of the human person and his or her relation to God and other humans, and the concept of symbol and the symbolic, this fourth section closes this chapter by examining exactly how grace operative in the symbolic exchange of the sacraments then manifests (or at least *ought* to manifest) as the Christian ethical life. The section begins with a brief outline of Chauvet's model of the church, which is that of a permeable yet defined community held together by shared reverence for and celebration of scripture, sacraments, and ethics. Following this, the section returns to the issue of consent, namely, the necessity of the human's consent to bodily mediation and, more particularly, the Christian's consent to the presence of the absence of God (and how this informs the Christian experience of scripture, sacraments, and ethics). Finally, after also emphasizing the corporate agency of the liturgical assembly in Chauvet's thought, the section will close by arguing that the sacraments—by sacramental grace—connect to ethics as the constitution of Christians as subjects of ethical action. The sacraments animate Christian identity

---

[70] Chauvet, *Symbol and Sacrament*, 183.

into Christian life in a symbolic exchange with God, the completion of which is the Christian ethical life.

Chauvet conceives of Christian identity and the church as constituted by the three poles of scripture, sacraments, and ethics. While scripture is not our central topic of discussion, it is worthwhile to note that by "scripture," Chauvet means not only the scriptural canon but also theological reflection (past and contemporary) and catechesis.[71] For Chauvet, this is the raw material for what becomes Christian practice in sacraments and ethics. The pole of scripture is how Christians access and receive (i.e., are formed by) the faith of Christians throughout the ages. The historical body of the church has spoken itself *into* what Chauvet calls scripture, and the contemporary church receives that gift as part of its own body. As David Power says of Chauvet, "He sees the church, and indeed the living assembly of worship, as the proper place in which the Word is interpreted and brought alive."[72] As the single human receives her- or himself from a context and history that precedes him or her, so the church receives itself from traditions that echo through history. Scripture is, for Chauvet, the first place the church receives itself.

The second of Chauvet's three poles of Christian identity, sacraments, also includes more than the official seven sacraments. For Chauvet, sacraments include all the actions of the church as church, as well as a number of devotional actions of individual Christians, such as prayer.[73] Sacraments, for Chauvet, are the loci for humankind's contact with God. This does not exclude Christians' contact with God through scripture but rather conditions it; the sacraments are the bodily mediation of symbolic exchange between God and humans, that is, the sacraments are the initial site for humans' reception of God informed by scripture. Additionally, while sacraments can include the devotional practices of individual Christians, sacraments are, at their base, intrinsically communal.[74] Just as scripture is not created individually, neither

---

[71] Chauvet, *The Sacraments*, 29.

[72] David Power, "The Word in Liturgy: Incarnating the Gospel in Cultures," in *Sacraments: Revelation of the Humanity of God*, ed. Philippe Bordeyne and Bruce T. Morrill (Collegeville, MN: Liturgical Press, 2008), 60.

[73] Chauvet, *The Sacraments*, 29–31.

[74] It is significant that the active entity in Christian liturgy for Chauvet is neither the priest nor the individual members of the gathered community but the liturgical assembly itself (Chauvet, *Symbol and Sacrament*, 183).

is the faith it inspires the province of an individual alone. From beginning to end, Christian identity for Chauvet is communal.

Chauvet ultimately uses the term "ethics" to connote all aspects of Christian living that might not be properly called sacraments. In his words, "Under the paradigm 'ethics,' we place all that pertains to *action* in the name of the gospel (therefore also, and even primarily, in the name of humanity)."[75] This means that, for Chauvet, life as a Christian means a life of ethics, which is the locus of the return-gift implied in the symbolic exchange of the sacraments. Chauvet does not delve too deeply into specific ethical questions or issues;[76] rather, he maintains that Christian ethical living is a necessary and organic product of Christian sacramental practice. For Chauvet, scripture provides a foundation for Christian faith, sacraments mediate that faith into Christian practice, and those Christian practices inform and animate Christian ethical life.

Chauvet is aware that while these three poles of Christian identity are all necessary parts of the church's makeup, each of them is prone to overemphasis, which can throw the church (conceived of as specific communities) out of balance. For example, Chauvet argues that the overemphasis on scripture can lead to fundamentalism.[77] Biblical fundamentalism is certainly one danger, but since Chauvet groups theological reflection together with scripture, fundamentalism with regard to certain teachings or figures can also be part of this temptation to overvalue scripture. Likewise for the sacraments, a lopsided favoring of the liturgical practices of the church can lead to a reduction of all elements of Christianity to their means of mediation.[78] If overemphasized, sacraments can become not just mediations of contact with the divine but also the gates of salvation, magic tricks that are effective only *ex opere operato* rather than effective by the action of God and humans within them. Ethics, for its part, also carries the danger of overemphasis, in

---

[75] Chauvet, *The Sacraments*, 31. Emphasis in original.

[76] This can be a problem in itself. Chauvet uses the term "ethics" to fit within and complete his system but does not apply the term to specific ethical practices in the way he does with specific sacramental practices (baptism, Eucharist, or others). Keeping in mind that this same critique could be made of this book, however, I believe this is more of an incompleteness than a weakness in Chauvet's project. It is not that he *couldn't* say anything about specific ethical issues; it is simply that he has not.

[77] Chauvet, *The Sacraments*, 40. Also Chauvet, *Symbol and Sacrament*, 174–77.

[78] Chauvet, *Symbol and Sacrament*, 174–77.

the form of idolizing either political activism or embodiments of personal charisma.[79]

Aside from these temptations (and the various forms each can take), Chauvet's tri-pole structure of Christian identity nevertheless provides a schematic for the symbolic order of Christian faith. The embodiment of this symbolic order in the sacraments and liturgy initiates the symbolic exchange between humans and God, but recall that such symbolic exchange requires humans' consent to the truth of bodily mediation. I return to the issue of consent here not because Chauvet's system ultimately hinges on it (I do not believe it does) but because thus far we have concentrated only on one half of Chauvet's concept of consent: consent to the mediation of reality *to* the human subject. This is an essential beginning point, because within the context of the sacraments, consent to the inescapability of mediation also constitutes consent to the presence of God's absence (something to which we alluded briefly above). The presence of God's absence for Chauvet connotes the fact that God in Christ is not immediately present to us humans, even in the sacraments. In fact, what *is* present in the sacraments is the space between humans and God, embodied in the very liturgical practice.

This does not mean that in the sacraments God retreats from humans who would otherwise have free and immediate access to the divine. The presence of God's absence is about the life of God in Christ, not the life of Christians in the church. Chauvet argues that the risen Christ is only present in the sacraments *as* the risen Christ, meaning for him that Jesus' physical, immediate presence is not possible.[80] Christ is absent, because Christ is risen; however, Christ is *really present*, because the symbolic exchange of the sacraments bears his presence as a gift to humans. In Chauvet's words, "Those who kill this sense of the absence of Christ make Christ a corpse again."[81] The import of this concept for Chauvet is twofold: first, it implies that the task of *becoming* the church is never-ending, because the mediation of the presence of God's absence is never "finished." As Chauvet argues, "The Church radicalizes the vacancy of the place of God. To accept its mediation is to agree that this

---

[79] Ibid.

[80] This point of Chauvet's has led some commentators to maintain that Chauvet insists too strongly on the presence of God's absence, which can lead to a weakened sense of God's initiative in liturgical practice (Philippe Bordeyne, "The Ethical Horizon of Liturgy," in Bordeyne and Morrill, *Sacraments*, 129–30).

[81] Chauvet, *Symbol and Sacrament*, 178.

vacancy will never be filled."[82] In this way, consent to mediation is additionally consent to the presence of God's absence and so also consent to the never-ending becoming of the church. The church is never a finished product. It is an ever-active mode and location of mediation.

The second reason Chauvet insists on this concept of the presence of God's absence is also the second half of his concept of consent: consent to mediation (of the presence of God's absence) *to* the human believer is also consent to mediation *through* the human believer. For Chauvet, becoming a Christian is a process that is never finished in much the same way that becoming the church is a process that is never finished.[83] Because the symbolic exchange of the sacraments is an exchange with the living God in the risen Christ, the exchange does not end when only the first part of the exchange (the sacraments themselves) is completed. This is the reason symbolic exchange always implies a response for Chauvet. Consent to mediation by symbolic exchange implies not only consent to *receiving* mediation but also consent to *becoming an instrument* of mediation.

Conclusion

This consent to both reception of mediation and being an instrument of mediation is the connection of sacraments to ethics in Chauvet. The two comprise two-thirds of the unified whole of Christian identity, but more than that, the two comprise a single, never-finished process that takes place in both the individual Christian and the church as a corporate body. I claimed above that, for Chauvet, sacramental grace ultimately constitutes a reception of one's self as a task. This task, the very makeup of the Christian believer in the context of the church, is animated by God's action in the symbolic exchange of the sacraments. Sacraments and ethics for Chauvet are not two "steps" in Christian life that theology ought to struggle to connect; they are two vestiges of the same process of symbolic exchange. Consent to mediation in one is consent to mediation in the other; that is, consent to mediation of the divine by the church in the sacraments also constitutes consent to mediation of the divine by one's self in ethics.

Beyond the importance for individual Christians of this identity of mediation in sacraments with mediation in ethics, it is worth noting

---

[82] Ibid.
[83] Ibid.

that the same identity holds true for the church itself in Chauvet's thought. In the liturgical assembly, it is the assembly itself (always with Christ as its presider) that acts as the recipient of grace in the symbolic exchange, rather than individual Christians who happen to be in a common space when the symbolic exchange happens. Just as the church forms Christians rather than vice versa, so the church acts in the sacraments as an entire assembly rather than as a group of persons who could have done the same thing individually. In this way, "the acting subject in the liturgy is the *ekklesia* as such,"[84] which implies that—since sacraments and ethics are two vestiges of the same symbolic exchange—the acting subject in Christian ethics is also (at least in some way) the church. This is the significance of Chauvet's use of the term "complex moral person" to describe the church. The communality of Christian identity goes beyond the liturgical assembly for Chauvet; it is a facet of every aspect of Christian life and identity. Because consent to mediation has both a receptive and an active aspect (receptive to the presence of the absence of God and active in the sense of allowing oneself to become an instrument of mediation), consent to the church's mediation is consent to embodying the church in every action.

Such embodiment goes beyond one's actions just "reflecting" in a positive or negative way on the church (though that would certainly be part of what embodying the church includes). Embodying the church in one's actions, that is, mediating what one has received in the sacraments into what one does in ethics, begins with how we embody the church in *our* actions. While Chauvet does not explore this extensively, his construction of Christian identity—and particularly the way he envisions sacraments and ethics—resists viewing ethics primarily as the actions of individuals. As the liturgical assembly speaks into existence the Christian body in which believers participate, so does (or should) the church speak into action the ethical lives of Christians. Individual believers share in a communal ethical life because they are not first individuals but first members of the Body of Christ. It is significant that Chauvet describes ethics as consisting "essentially in the agape between brothers and sisters"[85] rather than the "good behavior" of individual Christians. Ethics is about community, no less than sacraments are. If Chauvet's thought holds consistent from his thought on sacraments to

[84] Ibid., 183.
[85] Ibid., 279.

his thought on ethics, then blessing and woe, fault and renown, are all shared as the church before they are shared as individuals. The symbolic labor, inspired by the sacraments, is no less a corporate exercise than is the symbolic exchange *in* the sacraments.

This chapter began by surveying Chauvet's concepts of the symbol and the symbolic. Chauvet's thinking on these concepts was inspired at least partially by his problems with the way he reads Thomas Aquinas on grace, causality, and sign. Regardless of whether Chauvet's critique of Thomas is fair and accurate, the alternative he provides rests on three main points: First, the symbolic order connotes a non-instrumental, utterly embodied view of language and reality, in which symbols mediate reality to persons and the presence of persons to one another. Second, symbols cannot function outside the specific symbolic orders of which they are a part. Christian symbols cannot function as intended outside the Christian context, national symbols cannot function as intended outside their respective context, and the same with all symbols; the embodied nature of reality requires context in order for symbols to function. Finally, the truth of this embodied, mediated reality is not self-evident; it requires the consent of those who participate in it.

The chapter then moved into its second section in order to lay the groundwork for Chauvet's thought on sacraments and ethics by summarizing his theological anthropology. For Chauvet, the embodied, symbolic nature of reality dominates human existence. Humans exist as I-bodies, entities for whom bodily mediation is inescapable. Further, this bodily mediation is not individualistic. Before there is a subject who can receive mediation, there exists the milieu out of which grows that subject. The triple body of culture, tradition, and nature "speaks" the human I-body into existence, leading to an intrinsically communal makeup of the human person. With regard to the divine, this means for Chauvet that God is also mediated bodily to humans, through the symbolic order of the church. Exactly how that plays out was the subject of the third portion of the chapter.

The third section maintained that, for Chauvet, the bodily mediation to humans of the divine (i.e., sacraments) takes the form of what he calls a symbolic exchange. The symbolic exchange of the sacraments is the mediation of God's gift of grace to humans, which ultimately is a reception of self that requires what Chauvet calls a return-gift. This return-gift is not given back to God but given forward to other humans in the form of the "symbolic labor" of ethics. This is not a tit-for-tat exchange, according to Chauvet, but rather a process based on the logic of gift exchange, the same kind of logic that governs the symbolic order. Further, this symbolic exchange primarily takes place not between God and individual humans but rather between God and the body of the church. Just as humanity itself is intrinsically communal, so is the symbolic exchange between humans and God.

This point led to the final section of the chapter, in which the connection of sacraments and ethics was treated specifically. For Chauvet, sacraments and ethics comprise two-thirds of a three-part model of Christian identity (the third part being scripture) and ultimately flow one into the other. The sacraments lead to ethics for Chauvet, not because ethics is the "proper" response to the symbolic exchange of the sacraments (though it is that too, in a sense), but rather because ethics itself *is* part of the symbolic exchange of the sacraments. The mediation of God in Christ *to* the church is also the mediation of God in Christ *through* the church into the human community. In the sacraments Christians receive grace, but this grace is also a task, which implies action beyond the sacraments themselves. Further, just as the sacraments are primarily communal practices, so is ethics communal in Chauvet's thought. Far from an individualistic conception, Chauvet sees ethics as nearly mirroring the sacraments; what happens in the liturgical assembly happens also as the ethics of the Body of Christ. It is in this sense that Chauvet can say that ethics, the church's return-gift, service to others, are "the primary locus of worship."[86]

Having outlined the background of this project in the first chapter, and having drawn into focus the relevant portions of Luther's thought and Chauvet's thought for the project, we may now move to the goal of this book: a conversation between Luther and Chauvet on the connection between sacraments and ethics.

---

[86] Chauvet, *The Sacraments*, 169.

Chapter 4

Conversation between Luther and Chauvet

Introduction

At the outset of this conversation between Luther and Chauvet, it would be helpful to name exactly what our goals are and, additionally, what tasks this conversation will not achieve. Ultimately, the overarching aim of this chapter is to use the insights drawn from these two theologians to mutually enrich their theologies. Just as the Finnish School appropriated Orthodox insights and language that allowed previously overlooked emphases in Luther to come to light, this discussion uses the theologies of Luther and Chauvet to buttress each other, fill in gaps, and challenge tensions that appear more vividly by their juxtaposition. In order to do this, the chapter pursues three avenues of conversation: the importance of the gift for both thinkers' sacramental theology, the theology of the human person in the connection of sacraments and ethics, and the role of the community in that connection. While both theologians emphasize the importance of the concept of the gift for sacramental theology, Chauvet remains weak on both the concept of the human person and the divine character of grace operative within the person.[1] Consequently, as Luther is strong on these points, his theology

---

[1] This is not to say that Chauvet does not *have* a theology of the human person or that he does not think grace comes from God; rather, it is to reaffirm what was

111

will provide additional substance for these underdeveloped areas in Chauvet. Luther, for his part, tends to underemphasize the social character of ethics and even the social character of the sacraments in certain lights.[2] As a result, Chauvet's intrinsically communal theology of sacraments and ethics will help to enhance such weak points. In the process of pursuing these main points of conversation, this chapter will also include a number of corollary points of conversation between the theologians, ideally lending more weight to these central issues in the connection between sacraments and ethics.

Whatever the possibility for exchange of ideas between these two theologians, it is essential in this discussion to maintain the characteristic strengths of each one's thought. The goal of this chapter is not to unite these theologians (as if such a thing were possible) into an amalgamated sacramental theology that ignores their significant differences. It is one thing to draw inspiration from one figure in order to help explain or flesh out the thought of another; it would be something quite different to sweep aside their theological discrepancies in doing so. For example, Luther's emphasis on justification by divine imputation, his insistence that Christian righteousness is passive, and his formula of *simul iustus et peccator* all strike chords that do not necessarily resonate with Chauvet. Additionally, Chauvet's insistence on the necessity of (particularly ecclesial) context for Christian identity, as well as his place for scripture *alongside* sacraments and ethics as sources for Christianity identity, would not mesh well with Luther's *sola fide* or *sola scriptura*. That said, such differences do not negate the possibility of conversation. On the contrary, they make the conversation worthwhile. What follows is a gesturing in three directions of resonance and mutual enrichment

---

alluded to in chapter 3: Chauvet leaves open the question of what makes up the human individual and views grace as the gift of one's self as a task.

[2] There would certainly be scholars of Luther who would disagree here, seeing in Luther both a robust theology of social ethics and a necessarily communal sacramental theology; see, for example, William H. Lazareth, *Christians in Society: Luther, the Bible, and Social Ethics* (Minneapolis, MN: Fortress, 2001), or the entries in Timothy Wengert, ed., *Centripetal Worship: The Evangelical Heart of Lutheran Worship* (Minneapolis: Augsburg Fortress, 2007). Nevertheless, these emphases in Luther remain muted in comparison with their role in someone like Chauvet. Luther's emphases in sacraments and ethics remain, for the most part, on the relationship of the human to God. See, for example, Paul Althaus and Robert C. Schultz, *Ethics of Martin Luther* (Minneapolis, MN: Fortress, 2007), or James F. White, *The Sacraments in Protestant Practice and Faith* (Nashville, TN: Abingdon, 1999).

for the theologies of Chauvet and Luther. Ideally this conversation can serve in some way to foster similar conversations and engagement for those Christian theological traditions that claim these thinkers.

Common Basis for Sacraments and Ethics: It's All Gift

The springboard for the very possibility of fruitful conversation between Luther and Chauvet on the connection between sacraments and ethics is their emphasis on the role of the gift. For both theologians, sacramental theology has its core basis in God's gift giving.[3] Luther and Chauvet both stress that the most apt way of conceiving of the ritual relationship between humans and God is through the paradigm of gratuity, particularly the dependence of humankind on the free gift of God's grace. For Luther, as we saw in chapter 2 above, God's gifts of promise and presence in the sacraments realize justification in the human, uniting him or her with Christ present in faith. Analogously for Chauvet, the symbolic exchange initiated by God in the sacraments and through the liturgical assembly speaks the human into Christianity, bringing God's grace to bear on his or her life in community as a task, a symbolic labor.[4] This first section brings together these two views of God's sacramental giving, attending especially to the ways such views provide a basis on which to build the subsequent exchanges of ideas (i.e., sacramental theological anthropology and ethics, and communal ethics and the sacramental community).

Common Concerns, Different Approaches

While their ways of thinking differ concerning how the gift functions and what language they use to describe divine and human giving—presence and promise in Luther, and symbol and symbolic exchange in Chauvet—it is striking that Luther and Chauvet share at least one major reason for clinging to the concept of the gift: a mistrust of scholasticism, especially as they (rightly or wrongly) see it in Thomas Aquinas and the strains of theology he inspired. For Luther, scholastic theology as he encountered it tended to dogmatize theological opinion, or to make God's relationship with humankind a kind of system whose mechanisms

---

[3] God's action of gift giving is hardly limited to Chauvet and Luther. See, for example, Kevin Seasoltz, *God's Gift Giving* (New York: Continuum, 2007).

[4] Chauvet, *Symbol and Sacrament*, 442–43.

followed rules that could be described through careful reasoning.[5] The pervasiveness of such an approach to theology, whether it followed Thomas, Scotus, or Ockham,[6] led in Luther's opinion to a kind of domestication of God, or at least an overestimation of human faculties. For Chauvet's part, Thomas and the scholastic theology that followed him could not break out of its dependence on views of causality, which led to an understanding of grace that could be more mechanistic than gratuitous. Chauvet does not maintain that such a pitfall is unavoidable in either Thomas or scholastic theology, but he does question why causality should hold sway in sacramental theology and turns to the symbol and symbolic exchange (his way of conceiving of the gift giving between God and humans) as an alternative.

If suspicions of scholastic theology led both Luther and Chauvet to embrace the paradigm of the gift—or at least the centrality of gratuitousness and graciousness—as an alternate cornerstone for sacramental theology, their methods in doing so could hardly be more different. While Luther clung to the concept of the gift by rejecting (as much as he could) the influence of Thomas's appropriation of Aristotle[7]—a philosophical vision that was arguably the most influential in Luther's context—Chauvet clings to the concept of the gift exactly *by* engaging the influential philosophies of his context (Heidegger, Mauss, and Derrida, among others). What Luther intuited about sacraments and ethics based on his reflection on scripture and the patristic sources to which he had access—namely, that sacraments are gifts of God to humans, and the operation of God's grace makes Christian ethics possible—Chauvet develops by drawing on both theological and philosophical sources, ultimately articulating a theology of gift giving expressed through the concepts of the symbol and symbolic exchange.

This difference in approaches to philosophy brings with it more than just slightly different emphases regarding the concept of the gift in sacramental theology and ethics. Chauvet's reflection on the gift through

---

[5] See, for example, Luther's objections against the hegemony of transubstantiation in sacramental theology (*LW* 36:30–35), or his objections against *fides charitate formata* (*LW* 26:88–90). For a more objective view of these traits of scholasticism, see Ulrich G. Leinsle, *Introduction to Scholastic Theology*, trans. Michael J. Miller (Washington, DC: The Catholic University of America, 2010), esp. 2–5.

[6] Leinsle states that these three represent the three main bodies of scholastic theology (*Introduction to Scholastic Theology*, 3).

[7] As Luther articulated, "The Holy Spirit is greater than Aristotle" ("Babylonian Captivity," *LW* 36:34).

the language of symbolic exchange precipitates a far more developed understanding in his theology of exactly what the gift entails and what it does. Chauvet's work on symbolic exchange attends to how the giver and the receiver might interact in terms of presence, absence, and mediation, the ways that obligation relates to the gift without converting symbolic exchange into market exchange,[8] and specifically how the liturgical community participates in sacramental giving and receiving. In Luther's theology, most of these issues are either assumed or overlooked. For example, when Luther speaks of the gifts of Christ's promise and presence, he does not first treat the question of what it means for God to give anything at all. Questions of the very structure of gift giving and receiving do not find a place in Luther's writings; he more or less assumes that the idea of a gift is self-explanatory: it is by definition something that is received without cost.

Even though Luther does not attempt to define exactly how the gift works, he does try to explain how God's gift giving unfolds in the sacraments, albeit nearly exclusively by models and analogies. Luther explains God's gift of the promise of forgiveness of sins and eternal life, as we saw in chapter 2, by using the model of a testament that he draws from the words of institution.[9] Likewise, he uses models to explain the gift of Christ's presence in the Eucharist (for example, fire and steel both in a heated sword)[10] and reacts strongly against importing philosophical categories to attempt to explain it discursively. For Luther, God's action of giving in the sacraments—that is, exactly how God confers grace in the sacramental *means* of grace—is not necessarily a fruitful area for philosophical inquiry.

Taking into account Luther's hesitancy to employ philosophy in sacramental theology, we can still maintain that Chauvet's treatment of symbolic exchange falls in line with Luther's core conviction for the sacraments: the paradigm for grace is the gratuitousness and graciousness of the gift. Chauvet does not develop models for God's gift giving in the same way Luther does, but his structure of symbolic exchange is consistent with Luther's view of the gift. Chauvet's definitions of gratuitousness and graciousness, as well as how he conceives of presence

---

[8] Chauvet's point in this regard is that there is such a thing as obligation within the category of symbolic exchange or the gift, and such obligation does not imply categories of debit and credit.

[9] Luther, *LW* 36:37–41.

[10] Ibid., 32.

and absence, develop explicitly what can be read as implicit in Luther. Admittedly, such a reading of Luther in this light has not yet been done,[11] but this is one of the goals of this conversation—and one of the reasons for adopting the Finnish School as a hermeneutical lens.

The Finnish School and Reading Chauvet into Luther

The Finnish School of Luther Interpretation emphasizes the presence of Christ in faith and thereby the unification of the Christian with Christ. Given this lens, as opposed to the view of justification primarily by divine imputation, one can begin to see how Chauvet's view of the symbolic exchange in the sacraments meshes with Luther's under-standing of God's gifts of Christ's promise and presence. First, in Chauvet's view of symbolic exchange, what is exchanged is not only the gift itself but also the giver and the receiver.[12] In the case of the sacra-ments, the symbolic exchange initiated by God bears God's self to those who receive them. Particularly in the case of the Eucharist, this exchange of self implies God's uniting with the Christian. What is bodily eaten and drunk cannot remain separate from the one who eats and drinks it. Especially for Chauvet, who stresses that the bodily mediation of reality represents the true human situation, eating and drinking the gift of Christ's Body and Blood cannot but unite the believer with Christ. There is no more "real" unification than bodily unification. For the sacraments at least, what Chauvet means by symbolic exchange evokes what Luther means by Christ present in faith.

The second way the Finnish School allows Chauvet to be read into Luther's sacramental theology derives from the reason Christ is present in the sacraments for Luther. In Luther's view, Christ's presence in the sacraments—particularly in the Eucharist—is assured by scriptural revelation, but the *reason* Christ is present is for us humans. Christ's promises of forgiveness and salvation come to us humans as Christ's bodily presence because we bodily humans recognize reality that way. As Luther points out, a less intimate bodily experience—that of hearing the Word preached—is no less important for Christian life than the sacraments of the font or the altar. What is addressed to the entire community in preaching, however, is given to each particular member

---

[11] The closest thing can be found only tangentially in Gordon Lathrop, " 'Is That Your Liturgical Movement?' Liturgy and Sacraments in an Ecumenical Ecclesiology," in Bordeyne and Morrill, *Sacraments*, 101–14.

[12] Chauvet, *Symbol and Sacrament*, 106.

of the community in the Eucharist.[13] Such an encounter with the promises of Christ made present in his Body and Blood moves the idea of Christ present in faith from the world of cerebral belief to the world of bodily reception. This is not because Luther thinks God somehow "needs" the body in order to save, but rather because for Luther, God has chosen to save us embodied creatures according to the way we experience the world: bodily. Christ's real presence in Luther's theology is *for us* bodily creatures.

In this sense, Luther sees the embodied presence of Christ as something of a pragmatic decision on God's part (though this makes it no less remarkable or undeserved; rather, like the incarnation itself, God meets humans where they are). Christ's presence in the sacraments, and thereby also in faith, is salvific because it bodily bears the gift of Christ's promise to the Christian and unites him or her to the savior. *That* this is a unification and a reception of real presence is a witness for humans of Christ's relentless love and grace.[14]

That said, what Luther sees in this case as God's accommodation of humans' embodiment Chauvet elevates to the level of theological anthropology. Chauvet would not object to Luther's insistence that the bodily presence of Christ in sacraments and faith is important for us humans; however, he would claim that beyond importance, such presence is actually essential for humans' experience of the divine. For Chauvet, there is no such thing as a purely intellectual or spiritual appropriation of Christ's gifts, because the human intellect and spirit is always embodied.[15] As such, Chauvet's view of the necessity of bodily mediation fits squarely in line with Luther's conceptions of reception of and unification with Christ. The Finnish School's insistence on constantly

---

[13] Luther, "Against the Fanatics," *LW* 36:348–49.

[14] While it is certainly important to emphasize the love and gifts of God available in the sacraments, it is worthwhile to note that Lutheran liturgical theology has also stressed the "warning" contained in the Lord's Supper alongside the "welcome." See Gordon Lathrop, *Holy Things: A Liturgical Theology* (Minneapolis, MN: Augsburg Fortress, 1993), 128. While Christ's salvific presence becomes bodily a part of the Christian in the eating and drinking around the Lord's Table, that also means that Christians are bodily implicated in the sacrament. Christ's body becomes part of Christians' flesh, and his blood flows through their veins. In the Lutheran view, Christians *are* Christ to the world, not in a merely representative way, but in a real, embodied way. Christ's welcome to the sacraments, particularly the Lord's Supper, carries with it the warning that participants carry forward into their lives from the Lord's Table that same saving presence that they received there.

[15] Chauvet, *Symbol and Sacrament*, 146–49.

emphasizing Christ's presence in faith throws this into sharp relief in a way that the more traditional interpretation of justification in Luther as divine imputation cannot. Where divine imputation tends to stress the distance between humans and God, the Finnish School stresses the closeness of Christ to the human in justification as unification. In the sacraments therefore, according to both Chauvet and Luther as viewed through the lens of the Finnish School, Christ comes to humans in the way that is most apt—bodily—and gives himself to particular Christians in the context of the liturgical assembly.

Possible Objections Explored

At this point one might object: doesn't Chauvet's absolute view of the body and its mediation implicitly make the claim that God cannot save except bodily? Effectively, doesn't Chauvet's use of philosophy in order to define the human condition as irreducibly embodied ultimately make the same "mistake" (as Luther would see it) as Thomas and the scholastics? Hasn't Chauvet allowed his anthropology to usurp theology? While it might be possible to read Chauvet in this way, one ought to note that Chauvet's stress on the embodied nature of humanity is at least as much phenomenological as ideological.[16] Chauvet's response to this question would likely be, "What aspect of human experience could *not* be utterly tied to the body?" One would be hard pressed to provide an answer that remains consistent with contemporary phenomenology and human science. Acting, moving, thinking, and feeling are all tied to the body and are made possible by it.[17] No less in theology, then, Chauvet would argue, is the body the vehicle for reality.[18]

---

[16] Chauvet is hardly the only figure to stress a phenomenology of the body. For others who neither figure into Chauvet's theology nor draw from it, and who yet have worked extensively on phenomenologies of the body, see Robert Sokolowski, *Phenomenology of the Human Person* (New York: Cambridge University, 2008), or Mark Rowlands, *The New Science of the Mind: From Extended Mind to Embodied Phenomenology* (Cambridge: Massachusetts Institute of Technology, 2010).

[17] The emerging field of somaesthetics bears witness to how completely much of contemporary thought on the body has rejected the idea of some internal "self" separate or even distinct from physicality. See Richard Shusterman, *Thinking through the Body: Essays in Somaesthetics* (New York: Cambridge University Press, 2012), or Giovanna Colombetti, *The Feeling Body: Affective Science Meets the Enactive Mind* (Cambridge: Massachusetts Institute of Technology, 2014).

[18] Chauvet's insistence on this necessity of the body would be distinct from other phenomenologists and scientists in that he grounds his insistence on the concepts of the symbol and the symbolic rather than on the methodologies of the human sciences.

Even if Chauvet's emphasis on the body does not violate Luther's principles with regard to philosophy, however, one could also object that while Luther focuses on the reality of Christ's presence in sacraments and faith, Chauvet's concept of presence is always tied to absence—a concept that Luther does not attach to Christ. For Chauvet, even though Christ's presence is necessarily mediated bodily, the fact that it is *mediated* indicates a space between Christ and the Christian—in Chauvet's words, "the presence of the absence of God."[19] This objection presents probably the largest challenge in creating common ground between Chauvet and the Finnish School. If Christ and the believer are really united in Luther as the Finnish School maintains, how can that evoke the kind of absence that is central to Chauvet's view of divine presence? How can unification admit of a space of absence between the parties who have been united?

Before answering this question directly, one ought to take account of the reasons Chauvet and Luther speak of presence to begin with. Rather than being opposed to Luther's concept of Christ present in faith through the sacraments, Chauvet's idea of the presence of Christ's absence can actually be read to serve the same theological purpose that Luther's emphasis on presence does. That is, they both serve to highlight how humans sacramentally experience Christ. As we have seen for Luther, Christ's presence is the mode of God's giving the promises of forgiveness and eternal life, which is itself a gift. It is a gift not only because it comes at no cost to us humans but also because it is even available at *all* for us humans. Christ's presence in faith is made manifest by Christ's presence in the bodily celebration of the sacraments, the mode according to which the gospel addressed to the community becomes embodied in each individual of the community. Similarly for Chauvet, the presence of Christ's absence serves to facilitate the symbolic exchange of the sacraments. This is not because there is some "more complete" divine presence that we humans ought to be able to apprehend; the sacramental presence of Christ's absence is what it is for Chauvet exactly *because* that is how we humans can experience Christ. It is not a limitation as Chauvet sees it but rather a means, very like Christ's presence is for Luther.

In more direct response to the question of how unification can include absence, first it is essential to realize that the unification in faith that the Finnish School proposes is not the same as the temptation of immediacy of which Chauvet is suspicious. For Chauvet, the presence

---

[19] Chauvet, *Symbol and Sacrament*, 178. Italics removed.

of Christ's absence does two things: first, it is an affirmation of the fact that we humans do not have immediate access to Christ any more than we have immediate access to the rest of reality that surrounds us.[20] The truth of the bodily mediation of reality includes the truth of the bodily mediation of Christ in the sacraments, which means Christ is distant just as he is present. Second, however, Chauvet's emphasis on the presence of Christ's absence serves to drive home the distinction between the sacramental "already" and the "not yet."[21] The temptation of immediacy extends to the temptation of an overly realized eschatology or, on the level of the individual, an overly realized mysticism. For Chauvet, the presence of Christ's absence is a safeguard against thinking that we humans have either immediate access to creation or immediate access to the divine.

In this light, Chauvet's concept of the presence of an absence does not militate against the Finnish School's concept of unification with Christ present in faith—at least not in its central aim. This is not, however, the same as reflecting or resonating with it. For that, we ought to look at the Finnish School's interpretation of Luther's *simul*.[22] If Chauvet's zeal in attending to absence within Christ's very acts of presence is based on his concern for guarding against an illusory immediacy between Christ and Christians,[23] then in order to preserve a common basis with Luther, Luther's doctrine of the human as both sinner and justified would provide the necessary complement to his view of unification with Christ in faith. Luther's *simul* is his own way of accounting for the same kinds of trouble Chauvet sees with immediacy: presumption of unrestricted access to—and thereby a kind of ownership of—Christ's righteousness. For Luther, justification as unification does not *change* the human except by addition; the one who was only a sinner is, after justification, both sinner and justified. There is still a part of the human that is prone to sin—united to Christ but not wholly converted *into* Christ.

This is to say that, for Luther, there is a kind of absence within Christ's presence in faith. Christians are not united to Christ in such a way as to domesticate Christ; unification with Christ does not make Christ's presence subject to human choice and action, as if Christ's

---

[20] See Chauvet's rehearsal of what he calls the "triple temptation" of "the imaginary capture of Christ" (ibid., 175–76).

[21] Ibid.

[22] See Mannermaa, *Christ Present in Faith*, 55–62.

[23] Which it indeed seems to be; see Chauvet, *Symbol and Sacrament*, 175–76.

presence were *immediately* at Christians' beck and call. Just as Chauvet's presence of the absence requires of Christians a kind of letting-go (of immediacy and consent to mediation), so Luther's presence of Christ in faith implies a surrender, namely, to the passivity of Christian righteousness. Justification as unification—the reception of Christian righteousness as Christ present in faith—is not accomplished on Christians' own terms but on God's. This is another part of the reason that gift giving is the core of the sacraments for both Luther and Chauvet: humans cannot take Christ's presence or justification for themselves either by immediate access or their own action. Humans can only receive it as a free gift, given according to the bodily modes of human existence, but still *received*, not taken.

Receiving the Gift: Reading Luther into Chauvet

If we grant that Chauvet and Luther share a common cornerstone for their sacramental theologies in the concept of the gift, the question remains: do they share a common conception of what is given and received? This is the issue of grace, and while it is an important issue for both theologians, they both also tend to treat the term as multivalent. As we have seen thus far, Luther speaks of grace in terms of justification, Christ's presence, and God's favor (often meaning a number of these at once), and Chauvet speaks of grace as a presence, a task, and even an identity. Yet even though neither theologian rests on a single, systematic definition of grace, both treat certain themes as dominant in their language of grace. For Luther, according to the Finnish School, the central way of speaking about grace is as unification with Christ in faith. For Chauvet, the idea of receiving grace ultimately points to receiving oneself as a task. At first glance, these two might not seem to hold much in common, especially given Luther's suspicion of terms that, like the word "task," might be read to minimize the free nature of grace or to connote a way humans might be able to satisfy some requirement and make themselves worthy of grace. Even in light of that possible objection, however, there remains common ground between Luther and Chauvet on how they conceive of grace.

To begin with the thorny issue, what exactly does Chauvet mean that in grace the Christian receives her- or himself as a task? We saw in chapter 3 that such reception of a task is the final operation of sacramental grace.[24] Christians receive the sacraments, and in the sacraments

---

[24] Chauvet, *Symbol and Sacrament*, 442.

they receive the one from whom they come (God in Christ), and in that reception they also receive the task of ethical life as Christians. From the standpoint of Luther, this operation could be read in two ways. First, one could read this operation of grace as a kind of "after the fact" works righteousness. With his relentless emphasis on the fact that humans cannot by their own power do anything to merit, achieve, or otherwise become worthy of grace, Luther could argue that by speaking of "task," Chauvet inserts ethical requirements into an operation that remains foreign to the very concept of requirements. After all, we just established that both Luther and Chauvet base their sacramental theologies on the idea of the gift. How can Chauvet speak, then, about a task included in the free gift of sacramental grace?

The second way Luther could read Chauvet's idea of receiving oneself as a task by grace would be to see within that idea a reflection of his own emphasis on unification with Christ. As the Finnish School interprets Luther, Christ present in faith represents a newness of Christian life, albeit a new life as *simul iustus et peccator*. The business of the Christian living out that *simul* is done united with Christ, divinized in a certain sense, and as such the Christian lives as Christ to the world.[25] Christians are freed by grace *for* this life, but the concrete embodiment of that life plays out as the life of a justified sinner. That is to say, the *simul* acknowledges that Christians' new life united with Christ is not an easy one in which ethical clairvoyance and actions are guaranteed. Rather, life as a sinner united with Christ is the life of someone constantly faced with the *task* of remaining passive to Christ rather than active against him. Christian righteousness is a gift received passively, but the life *of* Christian righteousness is a task *accomplished* passively.

This second way Luther could read Chauvet's concept of grace as task also brings to bear the importance Gerhard Forde saw in retaining the death and life language of justification, over and against the legal metaphor for salvation. Within the legal metaphor, a task can only be conceived of as something required of someone, and the danger implicit in such a conception is that accomplishing said task, even partially, could be seen as "to the credit" of the person charged with the task. Within the legal metaphor, accomplishing a task would earn a kind of merit— something that is anathema for Lutheranism as a whole. If grace and

---

[25] Luther, "The Freedom of a Christian," *LW* 31:367, and Mannermaa, *Christ Present in Faith*, 49–51.

the task Chauvet sees as integral to it are conceived of in terms of death to sin and life in Christ, however, the problems of earning and merit dissipate. The "task" of which Chauvet speaks could be read simply as the task of living this new life in Christ. As Forde points out, quoting Paul, "How can you who were dead to sin now live in it?"[26] Living itself is a kind of task. As in the Finnish School, the *simul* plays an important part here, as the new life of the Christian does not obliterate the old human but subjects the old human to life in Christ. This is Forde's view of sanctification, "the business of getting used to justification."[27] Life moving forward from justification *is* a task, but not one that determines justification itself. It is the task of constantly moving from death into new life in Christ. Grace does not move us from life in sin to death in grace but rather from the death of sin to life in grace.

This is one of the rare places where Forde's Radical Lutheranism and the Finnish School stand together. That in itself is telling, as these two interpretations of Luther rarely resonate with each other. Consequently, their resonance in this regard is not insignificant; it emphasizes the importance in Luther's sacramental theology of what Gordon Lathrop calls the "welcome and warning."[28] Justification is free, grace is free, and the sacraments are free; life itself is free in Christ, and we humans are welcome to it. We humans are warned, however, that that life in Christ is a life of Christian ethics, lived out as the task of remaining passive to Christ's activity within us. Grace and the sacraments in this way do not constitute an ethical "get out of jail free" card; they bring with them a life sentence. What Chauvet calls the task included in grace, Luther would simply call sanctification: the task of life moving forward from justification as *simul iustus et peccator*.

Reading into Chauvet the Lutheran views of grace as unification with Christ or new life in Christ can illuminate his thought on grace as a task in a way he does not himself develop. Specifically, what can initially sound (especially to Protestant ears) like the insertion of requirements or "strings attached" into God's action and presence in grace could be nuanced with the help of Luther. By interpreting grace as the task of

---

[26] Forde, *Justification by Faith*, 11.

[27] See Forde, "A Lutheran View of Sanctification," 13–15.

[28] Lathrop, *Holy Things*, 128. Lathrop himself would not likely identify completely with the Finnish School and still less likely with Radical Lutheranism, which emphasizes again the overarching importance of this idea in Lutheran sacramental theology.

embodying Christian righteousness rather than as the task of progressing *toward* Christian righteousness, Chauvet's emphasis on the integral connection between grace and ethics is preserved and does not carry connotations of works righteousness or the requirement of merit for salvation.

Reading Luther and Chauvet in light of one another on the gift and grace has established some common bases between their approaches to sacramental theology and its connection to ethics, but these topics in themselves do not attend to theological weaknesses each theologian would see in the other. Thus far, we have attended to how grace comes to and works through the human person, but we have largely ignored the fact that even speaking *of* the single human person presents problems for Chauvet. Likewise, we have explored how grace as a task can connote a life of Christian ethics but in doing so have essentially assumed the single Christian person as the locus of that task—an assumption to which Luther might not object but that would give Chauvet pause. Having established a common basis held by Chauvet and Luther on sacramental grace as gift, this discussion now moves to using that basis as a bridge over which to exchange ideas that can challenge each figure's theologies of sacraments and ethics and also supply insights to strengthen them.

Theological (Sacramental) Anthropology and Ethics

Luther and Chauvet both base their sacramental theology on the concept of the gift, and the way both theologians connect sacraments to ethics depends on God's gift giving, but who or what exactly is the human who receives these gifts? If reception of Christ in sacramental grace is the basis for the task of a life of Christian ethics in both Luther and Chauvet, who or what is the human who actually lives that life? The reason this question is important goes beyond the fact that Luther and Chauvet would not necessarily agree on the makeup of the human person. While that area of difference simply *by* its difference constitutes an attractive possibility for creative conversation, the importance of the question of the human person for the connection of sacraments and ethics is ultimately this: the answer one gives to such a question forms the practical implications of the connection between sacraments and ethics. The theological connection of sacraments and ethics in Luther and Chauvet is based on the gift, but that connection does not find embodiment or translation into practice except through the ways it interfaces with their views of the human person.[29] In this light, this section of our discussion focuses on two ways the theological anthropologies of Chauvet and Luther present challenges to how they conceive of sacraments and ethics: the danger of ethical and ecclesial complacency in the case of Chauvet and the danger of ethical despair or flippancy in Luther.

Chauvet: Is There Such a Thing as the Human Person?

In order to tease out the danger of complacency implicit in Chauvet's view of theological anthropology, it is helpful to begin with the question alluded to in chapter 3: what, in Chauvet's view, actually is the human person? Does he have an idea of what such an entity is, or does his communal theological anthropology preclude such an idea? The reason such a question is even possible is Chauvet's concern to depart from anything that resembles the "autonomous individual" that the Enlightenment so favored. In his zeal to replace what he sees as this mistaken concept with a relational anthropology that takes full account of the constitutive role of one's context, Chauvet essentially leaves open the question of what this human is for whom context and relations are so essential. Such a lacuna is not fatal for his theological project, but without development and nuance, Chauvet's human person can be left as a kind of drone, influenced and ultimately driven by the corporate bodies that surround and speak her or him into existence.

As chapter 3 outlined, Chauvet's theological anthropology is centered on the truth of the bodily mediation of reality and the intrinsic communality of human existence. The triple body of culture, tradition, and nature speaks the human I-body, and its own speech as the I-body is conditioned by the corporate bodies of which it is a part. In the ecclesial context, for Chauvet it is the church that forms Christians, not the other way around.[30] Christians depend on the communities of which they are a part for mediation of reality—mundane and divine—and also for engagement with that reality. The human community or communities that

---

[29] One might point out that ethics itself ought to be thought of as the practical implications of sacramental theology. Such a claim still serves to make our point, however: sacraments, ethics, and the way they connect as God's gifts all assume a particular view of the human person and his or her relationship with God and other humans. As such, the bridge from the practice of *living* those relationships to the theory behind them is theological anthropology.

[30] Chauvet, *The Sacraments*, 31–32.

surround and contain the human person provide that person with his or her possibilities for speech, action, and even thought to a certain extent.[31] The systems of symbols (particularly the sacraments) that inform the ways that Christians approach their reality in fact do much more than inform that approach for Chauvet—they are the condition on which that approach depends.

The problem with this approach to the Christian person is twofold: first, it assumes that there is some entity called the human I-body that receives bodily mediation without actually developing an idea of what the *I* portion consists. The very structure of the term Chauvet chooses— I-body—suggests that there is some distinction between that which is strictly and only bodily and some other aspect of the human person that one might call the self (for lack of a better term). Unfortunately, nearly every possibility Chauvet has to explain what this "self" might be he uses to explain that such a self does not exist.[32] There is no "pure interiority," no human self that is separate from the body for Chauvet; he holds fast to that line from Nietzsche, "Body am I, and nothing besides."[33]

Taken to its extreme, this hyper-stress on the embodied nature of humankind leads to something like biological determinism. Especially combined with the fact that for Chauvet the human I-body depends for its existence and speech on the triple body that precedes it, the question of what is the *I* portion of the I-body becomes the question of how the human is not in the end only a biological mechanism. The human may be in his view a wonderful and complex mechanism, but still a mechanism utterly dependent for its speech, action, and thought on forces that are not its own. Chauvet would almost certainly object to this characterization of his thought, but, as it is, his theological anthropology does not include any potent guard against such an interpretation. The closest Chauvet comes to addressing this problem is when he speaks of language (and also the sacraments) as both *instituting* and *instituted*, meaning that while language institutes reality and is prior to those particular beings whom it speaks into existence, it itself has also been instituted by those who embody it.[34] Even in this case, however, Chauvet resists affording the human person any substance or potency except as

---

[31] At least to the extent that thought depends on language, the person therefore depends on the sources of language (the preexistent human communities and symbolic systems that give rise to it) for the possibility of thinking.

[32] See Chauvet, *Symbol and Sacrament*, 96–100, 146–49.

[33] Ibid., 149.

[34] Ibid., 377–79.

being the location of a particular embodiment of the prior language that makes him or her up.[35] In Chauvet, the body is everything, which (without clarification) leaves the human as an animal whose rationality and spirituality cannot be discerned from its physicality.

To be fair, we ought not advocate for an ethereal self that is wholly independent of both body and contextual influence. Such an idea has been rightly and heavily critiqued (and Chauvet's thought assumes these critiques).[36] Nevertheless, wariness of such a concept is not necessarily the same as rejecting interiority or the human self altogether. The makeup of the human need not be either mind or body (as if the mind were not bodily or the body were independent of the mind); the human is both-and, as Chauvet attempts to evoke with his term of the I-body. He is just missing substance for the *I*.

The second problem with Chauvet's theological anthropology depends on the first and leads to what we have called the danger of complacency. If the human I-body depends for its speaking and living on the triple body that precedes it, then there remains little mechanism or possibility for the I-body to challenge the *status quo* of the corporate bodies that make it up.[37] Within this conception, the human cannot

---

[35] In Chauvet's words, "this instituted [language] is not simply one law among others, but rather the original space of all institutions and all culture. Subjects emerge from this primordial subjugation to a language already there. Language set to work in *discourse* or the language act is the instituting mediation of subjects in what is both most social and most singular about them because the formal architecture of their tongue is assumed by each person in a *new* way, an unprecedented event: an event of language" (ibid., 377, emphasis in original). Further for Chauvet, the law of language is uniquely powerful *precisely because* "no one ever decreed it as such" (ibid., 377). Even in the "act" of instituting, Chauvet limits the human subject to the role of the stage on which the linguistic triple body plays out, rather than that of an actor who might exert some influence on the story.

[36] Though it is important to note that recent work in philosophy and science has tended not to reject outright the idea of the self as a center of human agency but rather to connect that center of human agency with its physical components, causes, and effects. See Jason D. Runyan, *Human Agency and Neural Causes: Philosophy of Action and the Neuroscience of Voluntary Agency* (New York: Palgrave Macmillan, 2014).

[37] I use the term "corporate body" here to connote the bodies that surround, inform, and speak the human I-body. Essentially, corporate bodies are those overlapping communities that make up the triple body that ultimately speaks the human into existence. One's ecclesial community, political community, social community, etc., I would term as corporate bodies, as they are particular yet overlapping systems of symbols, meaning, values, presuppositions, and everything else that makes bodies "speak."

prophetically act against his or her community, or creatively reject the ways the community operates, because the human is the location of a language-event, not the *actor* in a language event.[38] What little possibility there is for the human to work for change exists only as the speech of one corporate body working through the human I-body in order to critique another corporate body. For example, one's passion for working for social justice might spring from the ecclesial community of which one is a part, or from social experiences derived from encounters with family, friends, or strangers, or from the political community with which one identifies. Whatever the source or sources, Chauvet's conception of the human precludes the idea that one's work or the reasons for it could derive from one's self.

On the surface this is not necessarily a problem. Work for justice or structural change and improvement is not itself impossible; what is impossible is the idea that such work results from anything other than the corporate bodies that make up the human person. Where this becomes a problem is with the realization that because of the primacy of the body and its communal determinants, the person her- or himself is not ultimately responsible either for the convictions that led her or him to act, *or* for the actions themselves. How *could* the person be responsible, since the *I* portion of the I-body is not distinguishable from the body that depends utterly on its context for its existence? Since the triple body speaks the I-body and not the other way around, what a human does is ultimately explainable by the network of relationships and experiences (always communal) that have made the human into who he or she is. Beyond biological determinism, this is social determinism.

It is likely Chauvet would object to this way of reading his view of the human person as well, and with similar vigor. Nevertheless, the reason for pointing out this issue remains the same: Chauvet does not include in his theology a concept that could be used to guard against it. Further, even if the primacy of communality for the makeup of the human person does *not* lead at last to social determinism,[39] it can lead to ethical and ecclesial complacency. If the fundamental anthropological

---

[38] Chauvet, *Symbol and Sacrament*, 377. It is also significant for this point that, for Chauvet, the liturgical assembly does not gather as human subjects (in his words, "individual *Is*") to celebrate a communal set of rituals; rather, the assembly itself is a "complex moral person," keeping active potency alien to the particular human subject, if there is such an entity (ibid., 183).

[39] This remains something of which I am not convinced.

concept is the human as a kind of conduit for the speech of the triple body, what imperative is there to pursue ethical action? One's actions are inspired and take place organically, because there is no other option. This is not an abdication of responsibility, because personal responsibility in the first place requires an anthropology that includes some content for what the human person is. Further, in speaking especially of the church, the Body of Christ, this stress on the primacy of the community saps the person's ability to challenge ecclesial injustice because in Chauvet's conception, the ecclesial body is exactly that body which formed the person's idea of justice to begin with. Rather than resignation to injustice within the church, this theological anthropology connotes blindness to it.

These problems in Chauvet's theological anthropology could benefit from some of Luther's insights (the task to which we now turn), but it would be false to suggest that prescribing a dose of Luther would serve as a cure-all for these tensions. What assistance Luther can provide can only be imported via the bridge of common convictions we outlined above, namely, the importance of the gift and grace for the connection between sacraments and ethics. That said, one of Luther's strengths that bears on this discussion is the perseverance his work affords the human person even in the context of being unified with Christ in faith. For Luther, the integrity of the human person's identity endures even through the process of death to sin and rising to new life in Christ. The *simul* stresses the gravity of human action and identity (particularly sin) in that the identity of the human as sinner is left intact throughout justification and union with Christ. Luther can stress this perseverance of the sinful human's identity even while taking on Christ basically without reference to the human's context. Whether or not that human relies on his or her context for either the old identity that dies to sin or the new identity received through the sacraments is not an important question for Luther. Rather, what is central for Luther is *that* the human dies to sin and rises to new life united with Christ in faith. Whereas Chauvet seems to lack a substantive identity for the *I* of the human I-body, Luther has two: the sinner and the justified human.

This is not to suggest that Chauvet ought to adopt Luther's *simul* in order to head off the two problems we've mentioned. Rather, this is to ask the question of what exactly allows Luther to both affirm the gift and grace in some of the same ways Chauvet does and yet also to speak of the human as an entity in ways that Chauvet views with suspicion. One of the obvious reasons, of course, is that Chauvet is writing in an era and context in which emphasis on the role of community and embodiment is far more pronounced than in Luther's context, but I suspect there is more to it than that. The central reason that the single human person is essential in Luther but nearly a nonentity in Chauvet is that, for Chauvet, the single human person is not the primary actor either ecclesially or ethically (as opposed to Luther, for whom Christ active within the person *is* the primary source of action). In the sacraments, for Chauvet, it is the liturgical assembly who is the acting agent, and, as we concluded in chapter 3, his ethics resist definition as the actions of individuals; instead, ethics for Chauvet connote the actions of communities.[40]

This is to suggest that, for Chauvet, even though he speaks of the I-body as his central definition of the human, the lacuna of what exactly *is* the human *I* may be intentional. Or if it is not intentional, it is still instrumental for the way Chauvet connects liturgy and ethics. As a result, an attempt to import from Luther a concept of the single human person, even on the basis of grace and the gift, would transform Chauvet's theology into something it is not. Chauvet's view of theological anthropology, with its stress on sacraments and ethics as actions of the community rather than the persons in the community, must stand on its own without help from Luther, problems and all, or risk compromising the theme that makes it what it is: the necessity of communal, bodily mediation.

That said, Luther's view of the human person still has something to contribute to a consideration of Chauvet's theological anthropology. It provides a counterpoint, something incompatible and yet parallel, useful as an alternate model of how sacraments and ethics operate. As Chauvet himself points out, his project was never about prescribing a new dominant interpretation of Christian identity. Rather, as Chauvet points out at the beginning of the constructive portion of his *Symbol and Sacrament*, "It is *one* model of the structure of Christian identity that we propose here," as opposed to the only adequate model.[41] His views have problems, even problems for which his system of thought may not be able to adequately account, but the solution—if it can be called that—would be to look to another model. If complacency and determinism are problems that cause one concern, Chauvet would likely suggest gleaning from his theology what one can, and then looking elsewhere to reckon with those issues. Luther's views of theological anthropology may not

---

[40] See our conclusion to chapter 3, and Chauvet, *Symbol and Sacrament*, 279–80.
[41] Chauvet, *Symbol and Sacrament*, 161. Emphasis in original.

exhibit the same problems for sacraments and ethics as Chauvet's do, but his theology is certainly not free of tensions either. It is to one set of these tensions that this discussion now turns, as well as to whether and how Chauvet's insights can be used to assist with them.

Luther: An Ethics of Passivity and Its Problems

One of the major problems concerning the connection between sacraments and ethics in Luther is, quite simply, establishing that there actually is a connection at all. By this I do not mean that Luther thinks the sacraments have nothing to do with Christian life. Rather, I mean that Luther would vehemently resist the idea that the sacraments "cause" ethical action,[42] or that ethics verifies or validates the justification accomplished in the sacraments, or other similar views. For Luther, the sacraments are places where God's gifts of promise and presence come bodily to particular Christians, unifying them with Christ in faith. The connection to ethics consists of letting Christ be active in one's life, that is, receiving Christian righteousness and remaining passive to Christ's action within oneself toward the world, particularly one's neighbor. This is what I meant at the conclusion of chapter 2 when I termed Luther's vision an "ethics of passivity." The active party in Christian ethics is Christ, united with the Christian in faith (accomplished in no small part by the sacraments). Luther's *simul* further explains this by maintaining that even in this unification the sinful human still endures, but he or she does so also as justified, one with Christ.

In light of this basic structure for how sacraments and ethics connect, two major problems emerge for Luther. First, such a conception of sacraments and ethics leaves essentially no room for creative human action. This is certainly by design in Luther,[43] but it can lead to a kind of despair or defeatism. If the human ethical task consists nearly exclusively of learning to be passive so that Christ can act, does that not then mean good works are ultimately impossible for Christians (and humans more generally)? If good works are in the end only actions of Christ

---

[42] Recall Luther's suspicion of the scholastics, and particularly his noting that justification does not necessarily lead to ethical progress or conversion.

[43] Luther is very clear that human active righteousness does not constitute Christian ethics. As a result, this exclusion of the possibility of creative human contribution outside the influence of Christ represents a kind of corollary to Chauvet's exclusion of the possibility of the action of the single human person. Both points can present problems for the theologies of which they are a part, but both are essential to their theologies.

united with the Christian in faith—and especially if faith is itself a gift from God and not a choice humans make—what worth remains in trying to be ethical? Is not humankind utterly defeated by sin, unworthy of anything except surrender?

In a word, Luther would answer yes—that is exactly his point. That is what his ethics of passivity means; complete surrender to the life of Christ received in faith through the sacraments. However, while this vision may come as good news and be freeing in some people's eyes at some times, it may be an occasion of despair for others or at other times. If the fundamental human choice is between sin on the one hand and Christ on the other, and "choosing" Christ is only possible by the free gifts of faith and grace, then we humans really are a miserable and damnable lot. Again Luther would probably affirm this, but this is far from an edifying view of humanity, and that is the problem. Theology in itself may not need to be edifying all the time, but it is useless if it is not pastoral (something Luther did understand quite well). As such, this particular view of Luther's may not be the ideal model to lift up in all situations, just as Chauvet's intrinsically communal ethics may not be either. The major difference in these two cases is that while Chauvet sets his model out as one way to conceive of Christianity among others, Luther rarely gives that caveat. That said, just as Luther could not directly alleviate the tensions in Chauvet except by providing an alternate model, neither in this particular case can Chauvet alleviate this weakness in Luther, except by similarly providing an alternate model.

Luther's ethics of passivity gives rise to another problem, however, for which Chauvet's theology *can* provide some amount of assistance: the problem of what might be called ethical flippancy. If we humans receive in the sacraments justification as unification with Christ in faith, and the connection to ethics is simply to allow Christ to act within and through us, then does the Christian "task" not consist basically in striving to not work too hard ethically? Ought one strive not to be too scrupulous, since ultimately ethical action can come only from the action of Christ and not one's own action? In a sense, this is the direction Luther goes with his theology, for example, when he writes to Melanchthon, "Be a sinner and sin boldly, but believe and rejoice in Christ even more boldly."[44] Trust in the effectiveness of grace—part (though not all) of what faith is for Luther—implies going about one's life with the

---

[44] Luther, "Letter 91, to Philip Melanchthon, Wartburg, August 1, 1521," *LW* 48:282.

conviction that while one will still fail on occasion, Christ's presence will ultimately work in and through one's life as the source of both justification and ethics.

In this sense, Luther's ethics of passivity connotes an abdication of one's ethical agency in favor of replacing it with Christ's. We humans can't do anything, so we shouldn't try; in fact, trying *itself* gets in the way of Christ's action within us, since the only thing we humans can actively do is sin. One should note, however, that objection against this kind of passivity—whether correct or incorrect—betrays an underlying assumption, namely, the assumption that ethics *ought* to include some kind of action or striving for action. If this objection comes across as something that should be self-evident, that should serve to illustrate just how deep the assumptions are that Luther attempts to challenge by his approach to ethics. As Forde pointed out, Christians all too easily can fall into the idea that they ought to be doing something,[45] and such an idea misses one of Luther's core insights: in the same way that Christians do not *do* anything to earn justification, so also Christians do not *do* anything in ethics except as united with Christ and passive to Christ's action.

While this kind of flippancy or dismissiveness with regard to the Christian's action in ethics is quite at home in Luther's thought, it (like the first problem with Luther to which we alluded above) is probably not the ideal way to approach ethics in every situation. Such a view might come across as immensely freeing for someone who is quite scrupulous as Luther was but, on the other hand, could be taken as a theological mandate for licentiousness for someone who lacks such scruples. In the latter situation, Chauvet's concept of grace as reception of one's self as a task would be helpful. We made the point above that one can read Chauvet's view of grace and task as resonant with Luther's *simul*, the life of the Christian moving forward from justification, united with Christ as both sinner and justified. In Luther's view, the task is to remain passive to Christ, and if sin abounds in one's life, then one ought to earnestly question exactly how passive to Christ one is. Luther's ethics of passivity is not an absence of ethics; it is a surrender to the ethics of Christ present in faith.

Put in Chauvet's language, this task is the task of Christian life in the world. If the language of passivity is unhelpful for one's view of ethics, then the language of task ought to help. Further, Chauvet's view

---

[45] Forde, *Justification by Faith*, 23.

of the task goes beyond what Luther might see as the primary Christian ethical call of love of neighbor. For Chauvet, the task of Christian life is the task of embodying Christ in the world *communally*, that is, primarily as a community of love that forms persons for ethics, *not* primarily as ethical persons who form a community of love. This task of living as the Christian community of charity would bring a different facet to Luther's ethics of passivity. Suddenly the focus is moved away from individual passiveness to Christ's action and on to communal embodiment of Christ's action. Ethical flippancy ought to dissipate, because, while looking at one's own ethical life in light of Christ might tend toward an individualism that minimizes the importance of one's actions for the community and the world, reaffirming the focus on community should return the urgency Luther sees in the connection of sacraments (justification) and ethics: how can you who are dead to sin now live in it?

To be fair, this translation of Luther's individual ethics to communal ethics[46] is less straightforward than this brief appropriation of Chauvet suggests. In fact, communal ethics in Luther is a thorny issue,[47] and while the resonance with Chauvet on the concept of the task of Christian life can assist in a small way, this discussion now turns to a more sustained engagement with the question: how can Luther and Chauvet enrich or challenge one another in their conceptions of communal ethics and the sacramental community?

Communal Ethics and the Sacramental Community

To return to the common bases of the approaches to sacraments and ethics in Luther and Chauvet that we outlined above, the gift and grace comprise the core of how sacraments and ethics connect. As we saw through the second section, however, Luther and Chauvet differ signifi-

---

[46] Here and following I intentionally use the term "communal ethics" instead of "social ethics" because while social ethics seems to connote specifically work for social justice and political change (for the development of this term in the US context, see Gary Dorrien, *Social Ethics in the Making: Interpreting an American Tradition* [Malden, MA: Wiley Blackwell, 2011]), I take communal ethics to include both social ethics and ethics particular to the ecclesial community: e.g., justice in preaching, worship, sacraments, church governance, etc.

[47] For one attempt at doing this, see George Wolfgang Forell, *Faith Active in Love: An Investigation of the Principles Underlying Luther's Social Ethics* (Minneapolis: Augsburg, 1954).

cantly in their anthropological emphases: Luther is most concerned with the gift of grace to the particular human person in sacraments and ethics, while Chauvet's intrinsically communal theology resists application to the particular Christian as an individual. Nevertheless, both theologians' views of sacramental grace (unification with Christ in Luther and reception of self as a task in Chauvet) give rise to ethics as the lives of Christians embodying Christ in the world. This confluence can throw light on two main issues that this discussion now works to address. First, embodying Christ in the world includes for both theologians a kind of consent (passiveness to Christ's action in Luther and consent to bodily/communal mediation in Chauvet). There are resonances between these views, but there are also areas of divergence, especially when speaking of consent to the ecclesial community. Second, the question of whether and how to work for social change takes strikingly different forms in Luther and Chauvet. For Chauvet, such an issue is almost a nonquestion; Christians embody Christ in the world and so ought to work to form the world toward charity. For Luther, however, this becomes a more convoluted issue, especially in light of events like his experiences of the Peasants' War and its aftermath. This section of the chapter draws together the strong points of each theologian's approach to communal ethics springing from the gifts of the sacraments and uses them to point out and inform their possible weaknesses.

Luther, Chauvet, and Consent

At the outset, we should note that the goal of this section is not to develop a consistent theology of consent based on Luther and Chauvet.[48] Rather, the reason the topic of consent bears on our current discussion is that what is, in Chauvet, necessary consent to the mediation of the body and community is, in Luther, necessary consent to the action of Christ in one's life. These are two quite distinct uses of the concept, but they come together when speaking of consent to the ecclesial community, the church. In the context of the sacramental community, consent to communal bodily mediation and consent to the action of Christ become nearly coterminous. This would create a problem in Chauvet's theology from Luther's point of view: consent to the necessity of bodily

---

[48] Consent as a theological topic has been treated well elsewhere. For example, see Aidan Nichols's connection of the topic to the existence of God in *A Grammar of Consent* (Notre Dame, IN: University of Notre Dame, 1991).

mediation in the context of the sacraments implies the necessity of consent to mediation by a human institution, and even particular humans (especially the clergy).[49]

While Luther does not specifically use the term "consent," this word sums up well what he means in speaking of the action of Christ in Christians as ethics. His ethics of passivity requires Christians to abdicate active righteousness in favor of receiving passive Christian righteousness. In this unification with Christ in faith, Christian ethics flows out as Christ active in the person but not as Christ *controlling* the person, as if ethics were some kind of game of divine mind control. For Luther, this choosing of passivity in order to receive Christ's action in one's life could rightly be called consent to Christ. Even in this case, however, such an action is not a good work that makes justification possible. Justification comes first, and the Christian's life as *simul iustus et peccator* then plays out united to Christ in faith. Only in union with Christ can the Christian consent to Christ's action.

Conversely, in Chauvet, the role of consent in Christianity is not consent to passivity or to Christ but consent to the necessity of bodily mediation—specifically through the communal bodies of which one is a part. In a sense, consent in Chauvet operates as an acknowledgment of the truth of the human situation, a kind of shedding the rose-colored glasses of immediacy. As a result, Chauvet would likely be leery of Luther's idea of consent to Christ, simply because such a consent is not built on bodily mediation. Luther's consent to passivity in Christian ethics certainly has a bodily component, as Christian ethics are not ultimately internal exercises but external acts of Christ in us, but this is the *form* of Christian ethics rather than the *condition* for it. In Chauvet's view, human existence does not include the possibility of immediate contact with Christ through which the human might be able to consent to Christ;[50] rather, humans can access reality (even and especially religious reality) only through bodily mediation.

Though his view of consent does not take into account the embodied nature of humanity in exactly the way Chauvet would like, Luther's

---

[49] It is worthwhile to note that Chauvet's system is (relatively speaking) not very susceptible to clericalism. Nevertheless, the necessity of the church for him would still be a point of contention for Luther.

[50] This is, in fact, the very falsehood and temptation—thinking of one having a direct line to Christ—against which Chauvet cautions. See Chauvet, *Symbol and Sacrament*, 171–73.

stress on the sacraments as means of grace does resonate with Chauvet's emphasis on mediation. In a sense, consent to the truth of bodily mediation in Luther is encapsulated by his reasoning for the importance of the sacraments: they are places God has promised to be, so why strive to receive the divine presence in other ways? As we mentioned above, this is something of a pragmatic theological move for Luther, while for Chauvet it is a tenet of theological anthropology. It is telling that Luther does not explicitly argue for a Christian's immediate access to the divine apart from the bodily nature of human reality.[51] While he does not treat embodiment with the same rigor Chauvet does, Luther nevertheless articulates a theology that is not opposed to embodiment.[52]

This area of resonance takes on a quite different hue when speaking of the embodied sacramental community, however. In speaking of the role of the church, the difference between Luther's pragmatic move and Chauvet's anthropological tenet takes on particular significance. Because the church, embodied as the liturgical assembly, is the context in which Christians are formed (for Chauvet) and in which Christians receive Christ's promise and presence (Luther), consent to bodily mediation and consent to Christ are very nearly the same action. Reception of Christian righteousness is a passive operation in Luther, accomplished in no small part by Christ's promise and presence in the sacraments. Formation as a Christian by the church is likewise for Chauvet an operation that occurs in the midst of the liturgical assembly and one through which one encounters and comes to embody Christ.

The conflict between these two views of consent to Christian formation or justification comes to light when one asks the question, does the Christian depend on the sacramental community in order to encounter Christ? For Chauvet, absolutely yes, and for Luther, absolutely no.

---

[51] Though, to be fair, Luther would not understand immediacy in the same way Chauvet does.

[52] This is not to say that dualism has no place in Luther. Certainly Luther opposes the spirit and the flesh with as much consistency as he maintains on any issue. This opposition parallels the opposition between the law and the gospel, however, not an opposition between physicality and spirituality. Luther is fond of dualisms, but most of them have little to do with setting the body and soul in conflict. See Carl E. Braaten, *Principles of Lutheran Theology* (Minneapolis, MN: Fortress, 2007), esp. chaps. 7 and 8; H. Richard Niebuhr, *Christ and Culture* (New York: HarperCollins, 1951), esp. 170–79; and Steven D. Paulson, *Lutheran Theology* (New York: Continuum, 2011), esp. 96–100 and 244–64.

Chauvet's entire concept of humanity revolves around the constitutive character of human community for the human person. As such, to speak of the human person's encounter with God apart from the mediation of the community would be nonsensical for him. For Luther, however, placing such importance on the mediatory role of the Christian community would represent a false limitation of God's freedom to come to humans in whatever ways God chooses.[53] The fact that God *does* choose to give Christ's promise and presence in the context of communal, bodily celebrations does not therefore mean that humankind is limited to those communal celebrations for contact with the divine. For Luther, God's work of justification cannot depend on any human action or construct—including the sacramental community of the church.

In Chauvet's defense, recall that he does not embrace the idea of strictly *extra ecclesiam nulla salus*; rather, he claims that there is "no *recognized* salvation outside the Church."[54] Chauvet would claim, however, that for the Christian outside of community there is no salvation. To be Christian, for Chauvet, one must consent to the bodily, communal mediation of the divine by the church. This would not be primarily a theological claim but an anthropological one for him; there is no such thing as a human who is not dependent for his or her existence on preexistent communities. The truth of communal bodily mediation of reality is just that for him: a truth about existence that can be either rejected in favor of untruth or accepted by one's consent to this truth. For Luther's part, it is likely he would read this necessity of communal mediation as a clever way to reaffirm the necessity of the visible, institutional church. Whether or not such a claim would be valid is a different question, but from a Lutheran point of view, it is convenient that Chauvet's anthropology would support an ecclesiology wherein the church mediates divine reality *to* individual Christians who must consent to it rather than one in which Christians who consent to Christ gather together to form the church.[55]

---

[53] Recall Luther's insistence that Christ can be found anywhere and yet that we humans ought to look for him in Word (addressed to the community) and Sacrament (addressed to particular humans) (Luther, "The Babylonian Captivity," *LW* 36:342–43, 348–49).

[54] Chauvet, *Symbol and Sacrament*, 180.

[55] This, of course, brings with it all the problems of being able (or not) to recognize and challenge ecclesial injustice that we alluded to in section 2 of this chapter.

Communal Ethics and Social and Political Activism

Beyond the issue of consent with regard to forming the sacramental ecclesial community and the Christians who participate in it, Luther and Chauvet would differ significantly on how and to what extent Christians ought to work to change their social and political contexts. This difference is, however, at least as much a result of their respective contexts and experiences as it is of the theological values behind it. Further, this specific difference is not one between two theologies that must stand as counterpoints, parallel to one another but without the possibility of an exchange of ideas. Instead, the differences between Luther and Chauvet on social and political action for change are informative for one another: Chauvet's thought can serve as a reaffirmation of the organic importance of Christian action for justice in societal structures that Luther often lacks, and Luther's thought can serve as a caution against an overzealous interpretation of Chauvet that could run the risk of putting the ends of social justice above the means for achieving it.[56]

For Chauvet, working for systemic change and reform in the social and political systems one inhabits would be a natural and even necessary embodiment of Christian ethics, formed as it is by the community of charity, the liturgical assembly. Ethics itself for Chauvet is as communal as his view of the human person, implying that Christian ethics in his view would include not only individual advocacy and activism but also systematic action as a community of faith. As such, Chauvet would view church organizations and advocacy groups, as well as more informal communal endeavors for social justice, as a central part of the Christian ethical mission. This is what receiving one's self as a task in grace would look like for Chauvet; the task is not simply the life of one Christian within society but rather the life of the Christian community in or as part of society. The corporate body of the liturgical assembly receives in the sacraments the task of living as Christ's body in intersections with the other corporate bodies of its context. Christian ethics for Chauvet occurs at the intersections of these communities.

In light of this high affinity of Chauvet's theology for causes of social justice and reform, one might well wonder how Luther could possibly object. What could be wrong with working to change unjust societal

---

[56] Chauvet would certainly not subscribe to the idea that the ends justify the means. Luther would point out, however, that the temptation to fall into that line of action—if not that line of reasoning—is ever present when speaking of Christian action.

structures? Luther's cautions in this regard come in two forms: one theological and the other more experiential. Luther's theological objection (if it can be called that) against striving for systemic political and social change stems from the way he views human life as lived in two kingdoms. Much has been said about exactly how Luther explains this concept,[57] but the main point for the purposes of our discussion is this: there is some legitimacy in the ability to use coercive and even violent action to govern the earthly kingdom, because the earthly kingdom is the realm of sin and the law. As such, citizens of the heavenly kingdom (Christians) ought not to mire themselves in the workings of the earthly kingdom except by being Christ to the world, that is, humans for whom love of neighbor is paramount. As this did not include working to topple the unjust structures of the Roman Empire for Jesus, neither need it include working to topple the unjust structures under which Christians find themselves living. Not for nothing is Luther often categorized as something of a social conservative.[58]

The second reason Luther would be suspicious of work for political and social change is his experience of and reactions to the Peasants' War in 1524 and 1525. While the causes of the revolt were complex, just as any major conflicts are,[59] one cause Luther saw as springing from his own writings: a literal interpretation of his explanation in "On Christian Liberty" that the Christian is subject to no one. In the face of what was seen (probably correctly) as widespread injustice and oppression, the peasants of Germany attempted to overthrow the aristocracy. Luther saw this as forsaking Christian values in order to achieve a political end and published a treatise harshly criticizing those he termed "rebels." Even the title Luther approved for this treatise is telling: "Against the Robbing and Murdering Hordes of Peasants."[60] That this treatise then

---

[57] An illuminating explanation can be found in William J. Wright, *Martin Luther's Understanding of God's Two Kingdoms: A Response to the Challenge of Skepticism* (Grand Rapids, MI: Baker Academic, 2010).

[58] A representative example of this would be George Malcolm Stephenson, *The Conservative Character of Martin Luther* (Philadelphia, PA: The United Lutheran Publication House, 1921).

[59] For more in-depth studies of the Peasants' War, see Tom Scott and Bob Scribner, eds. and trans., *The German Peasants' War: A History in Documents* (Amherst, NY: Humanity, 1991), and Michael G. Baylor, *The German Reformation and the Peasants' War* (New York: Bedford/St. Martin's, 2012).

[60] Martin Luther, "Against the Robbing and Murdering Hordes of Peasants," trans. Charles M. Jacobs, in *The Christian In Society III*, vol. 46 of *Luther's Works*, ed. Robert C. Schultz and Helmut T. Lehmann (Philadelphia, PA: Fortress, 1967), 49–56.

gave theoretical license for the aristocracy to carry out mass butchery in putting down the Peasants' War did not change Luther's view on the subject. In fact, in a later work further explaining his position, Luther reaffirmed his criticism of rebellion, claiming that it is the Christian's duty to "endure every kind of suffering"[61] rather than to resist it by force.

Given these objections, some interpreters of Luther have concluded that he has no place for resistance against tyrannical injustice. Such an interpretation has largely been debunked by figures like Dietrich Bonhoeffer[62] and Uwe Siemon-Netto,[63] but nevertheless the possibility of misinterpreting Luther in this way makes Chauvet's seamless connection between sacraments and communal ethics a worthwhile corrective. Further, this corrective from Chauvet is indeed something that fits within Luther's theology on the basis of his shared convictions with Chauvet concerning grace and the gift. For Luther as well as Chauvet, the sacraments connect to ethics by the gift of grace, that is, Christ's action within Christians and the Christian community. For Luther, the love of neighbor that Christ embodied becomes the love of neighbor that Christ enacts through Christians, which ought to include work for social justice. Further, as ethics for Chauvet takes place at the intersections of communities with each other, it would only be a small step to translate love of neighbor into the communal love of neighboring communities.

The caveat Luther would want to include, cautioning Chauvet's theology of communal sacraments and ethics, is one against violence. While Luther had no love for what he saw as the legitimate use of force by the state, for him such exercises of violence are qualitatively different from rebellion and revolution.[64] Because of the way Luther conceives of temporal power (i.e., the way he views the two kingdoms), rebellion always

---

[61] Martin Luther, "An Open Letter on the Harsh Book against the Peasants," trans. Charles M. Jacobs, in *The Christian In Society*, vol. 46 of *Luther's Works*, eds. Robert C. Schultz and Helmut T. Lehmann (Philadelphia, PA: Fortress, 1967), 70.

[62] Accomplished in both his life and in his works. See Eberhard Bethge, *Dietrich Bonhoeffer: A Biography* (Minneapolis, MN: Fortress, 2000), Dietrich Bonhoeffer, *Ethics* (Minneapolis, MN: Fortress, 2009), Dietrich Bonhoeffer, *Discipleship* (Minneapolis, Fortress, 2001).

[63] See especially Uwe Siemon-Netto, *The Fabricated Luther: Refuting Nazi Connections and Other Modern Myths*, 2nd ed. (Saint Louis, MO: Concordia, 2007).

[64] See Luther, "An Open Letter on the Harsh Book against the Peasants," *LW* 46:52–55, and Martin Luther, "A Sincere Admonition by Martin Luther to All Christians to Guard Against Insurrection and Rebellion, 1522," trans. W. A. Lambert, in *The Christian in Society II*, vol. 45 of *Luther's Works*, ed. Walther I. Brandt and Helmut

consists of illegitimate force attempting to overturn legitimate power. This could also be due in part to Luther's context of sixteenth-century Germany, but the strength of his point remains relevant: on what basis could Christians possibly take up violence to achieve the kinds of just ends for which Christ himself neither condoned nor participated in violent action?

Beyond the issue of the legitimate use of force versus illegitimate uses of force, it is worthwhile to note that systemic social and political change in Luther's time was rarely, if ever, nonviolent.[65] There is little reason to suspect that Luther conceived of the possibility that systemic change for social justice could take the form of anything other than violent resistance, and as a result he does not have a strong theology of communal ethical action for change. Rather, Luther's ethics of passivity focuses on the ethical action of Christ in and through the Christian individual, taking the form of the love of neighbor and suffering injustice with the same patience Christ exhibited.[66]

Chauvet for his part would not likely condone violent resistance, but the line between violence and nonviolence, and even the definition of violence itself, has become less and less clear in contemporary thought on the subject.[67] War and armed conflict certainly constitute violence, but are they the only forms of violence? Would economic coercion constitute violence? At what point would impassioned activism cross over into sowing social discord and unrest? Would bribery in order to achieve the passing of a just law (or the repealing of an unjust one) be an au-

---

T. Lehmann (Philadelphia, PA: Fortress, 1962), 51–74, and also Martin Luther, "Temporal Authority: To What Extent It Should Be Obeyed, 1523," *LW* 45:75–130.

[65] It is significant that while many histories of nonviolence include *calls* to nonviolence from throughout the Common Era (for example, Michael G. Long, ed., *Christian Peace and Nonviolence: A Documentary History* [Maryknoll, NY: Orbis, 2011]), histories of nonviolent *movements* tend to encompass history from only the Colonial Period on (for example, Stephen Zunes and Sarah Beth Asher, eds., *Nonviolent Social Movements: A Geographical Perspective*, [Malden, MA: Blackwell, 1999], or Sharon Erickson Nepstad, *Nonviolent Revolutions: Civil Resistance in the Late 20th Century* [New York: Oxford University, 2011]).

[66] Such a view of ethics, if taken absolutely, is at best dangerous. It can legitimize oppression, exploitation, and a slew of sinful structures and practices. In this light, it is essential to recognize that Luther's inspiration for espousing such a view is at least partially the *prevention* of violence, not the endorsement of it.

[67] See, for example, Hannah Arendt, *On Violence* (San Diego, CA: Harcourt Brace & Company, 1970).

thentic exercise of Christian ethics? We need not attempt to answer such questions here; rather, the point is to consider that while Chauvet's theology has valuable connotations for social ethics, would Luther's caution against the use of violence or other non-Christian means to achieve social ethics be well placed within Chauvet's project? Grace as a gift received in and through the Christian sacramental community is never violent, so neither can the actions of Christians embodying that grace of Christ in the world legitimately participate in violent means to their ends.

Conclusion

This chapter has attempted to develop ways in which the theologies of sacraments and ethics in Luther and Chauvet can enrich one another. Beginning with establishing a common basis in the gift and grace, the discussion argued that it is through this nexus (assuming the hermeneutic of the Finnish School of interpreting Luther) that the theologies can legitimately exchange insights without compromising their own central tenets. The second section of the chapter attended to tensions in Luther and Chauvet as they appear in their sacramentally formed theological anthropologies. In the case of Chauvet, Luther's theology provides a useful counterpoint to guard against complacency in the face of social or ecclesial injustice. For Luther, Chauvet provides a way of approaching ethics that would minimize the danger to draw from Luther either ethical despair or flippancy. The final section of the chapter worked to compare the theologians' approaches to communal ethics and social action, beginning with the issue of consent (to the mediation of the community in Chauvet and to Christ's action in Luther). Flowing from that discussion, the chapter ended by using Chauvet's theology to buttress Luther's fairly weak theology of social or political activism and by using Luther's theology to caution against the use of violence or unethical means in the pursuit of social justice that is ethics in Chauvet.

Conclusion

In conclusion, what are we left with? What has been accomplished, and what contributions have been made? The introduction laid out a central goal: to forge an ecumenical conversation on the connection between sacraments and ethics in which theological resonances would be named and developed and where the conversation partners might be able to draw from one another's strengths. I believe this book has accomplished that, at least in sufficient part to provide a basis and model for further such work in the future. The tensions in each theologian's thought have not been solved, nor has the book concluded with any overarching consensus on the connection between sacraments and ethics in Luther and Chauvet, but that was not the point of the project. The point was not to grasp at unity but to read each theologian in light of the other and to allow the insights of each theologian to speak to the tensions of the other. We have not been pursuing unity in thought, but there has been a unity of purpose. This purpose has been to move Luther and Chauvet, first, into conversation and, second, from facing each other across the conversation table to speaking side-by-side as sources for each other, providing mutual theological enrichment.

The book began this endeavor by situating the project within the larger field of liturgy and ethics, by outlining the central interpretations of Luther (particularly the Finnish School) that the book would follow, and by describing the philosophical milieu out of which Chauvet has written. The project then moved to a study of the connection between sacraments and ethics in Luther's theology, particularly in light of his view of God's gifts of promise and presence, his view of justification and unification with Christ, and his anthropological axiom of the human as *simul iustus et peccator*. A chapter on Chauvet followed, in which his theological foundations in the symbol and the symbolic, and his theological anthropology were summarized. The chapter then ended with an explanation of how symbolic exchange plays into Chauvet's sacramental theology and how that, through grace, enters his view of ethics as the lives of Christians in the world.

The fourth chapter began by naming a common basis for the approaches both Chauvet and Luther take to sacramental theology, namely, the gift. While Luther speaks of the gift in terms of promise and presence, and Chauvet speaks of the gift in terms of symbolic exchange, they both hold as a central concern the very foundation of sacramental theology in the gift of God's grace and its gratuity. This was the move to bring Chauvet and Luther to the same conversation table, to provide a nexus point for theological exchange; this was the bridge across the Tiber. To move Chauvet and Luther to the same side of the conversation table, the chapter named some tensions in their theologies in the connection between sacraments and ethics. In Luther, the emphasis on the passivity of Christian righteousness leads through unification with Christ to a kind of ethics of passivity, which can smother ethical zeal and turn to a kind of despair if it is not nuanced. Further, for Luther, social and political activism, even in the face of oppression, does not find much support in his theology. For Chauvet's part, his theological anthropology can be read in certain ways as rather hollow, which can lend itself to ethical complacency. Additionally, in Chauvet, the necessity of consent to bodily mediation can lead to a sapping of the prophetic role of the church in society, and/or of the prophetic role of the single Christian within the church.

Given these tensions in both Luther and Chauvet, each theology is poised to provide some theological help to the other. Chauvet's emphasis on the gift of grace as a task can help to temper Luther's insistence on passivity, and the resistance of Chauvet's conception of ethics to only the life and actions of single individual Christians can help infuse Luther's theology with a place for communal action for social justice. On the other hand, Luther's emphasis on the unification of the Christian with Christ can temper Chauvet's fixation on the necessarily communal bodily mediation of reality, and Luther's conception of ethics as Christ-in-us can reinvigorate the prophetic call that can become obscured in Chauvet's theology. In each case, the tensions are not necessarily resolved, but they are eased without losing the central insights that grow out of the tensions in the first place. Luther's *simul*, *sola gratia*, and *sola fide* do not dissipate simply because there might be an ethical task implied in the reception of the sacraments, or do they because communal ethical action is necessarily part of the Christian call in the twenty-first century. On the other hand, Chauvet's theological anthropology does not cave into immediacy simply because the Christian may be thought of as united with Christ, nor does the intrinsic communality of humanity and Christianity dissolve because in ethics Christ acts within Christians. These are places of possible enrichment, relatively safe from selling out one theology or the other.

Unearthing and developing these places of enrichment provides more than just a few talking points between Luther and Chauvet, however. The fact that their theologies might be read as able to share insights provides a possible new way forward in an area of ecumenical conversation that has stalled at a number of points: sacramental theology. In moving the conversation beyond understanding one another to striving to build one another up and appropriate from one another contributions that enhance one's own thought, unity becomes less of a goal and more of a byproduct. There is not in this exchange any decision to agree first or even to strive to reach agreement, and yet there is a kind of unity in the exercise itself. In this sense, this project is an example of trying to allow theologies to work together rather than trying to work theologies toward one another.

Springing from this model of ecumenical conversation as resonance and mutual enrichment are at least two possible veins for future work. The first would be systematically methodological. The book undertook its conversation with a general idea of ecumenical method and specific ideas of theological method (particularly in sacramental theology and theological anthropology), but developing this model as a schematic for further and altogether different ecumenical conversations was beyond the scope of the project. Working out a specific methodology or model for ecumenical conversation based on the example of this project may prove worthwhile, or it may at least serve to highlight implicit problems with the approach I have taken. Either way, this is a direction for further work based on this project.

The second area of possible future work would be in teasing out the practical implications both of this specific project and of the model of conversation it employed. With regard specifically to the connection between sacraments and ethics, one practical implication might be a greater emphasis on ecumenical collaboration in work for social justice, based on the connection held by both Luther and Chauvet between

God's gift giving and Christians' lives in the world. Such collaboration is not altogether uncommon already, but its theological warrant tends to be based on Christians' common baptism. This is certainly not a problem, but this project provides a similar basis for collaboration and goes beyond by drawing at least as much support from theologies of the Eucharist as it does from theologies of baptism.

As for the model of conversation, one might ask what could happen if ecumenical conversation partners were to take as a matter of course the ability both to draw from and to attempt to inform the theologies of their conversation partners? Certainly presumptuousness would be a problem at least initially, but tempering that would be the very point of putting aside the imperative to work toward unity and focusing instead on resonance and collaboration. Just as collaboration in work for social justice would *show* a kind of unity, so would collaboration in ecumenical theology *show* a kind of unity without first attending to it as a problem to be solved. This in itself would not dissolve ecclesial divisions, of course, but it would be one more way forward in the vast field of ecumenical work yet to be done. It is my hope that this book, formed as it is by the search for resonance and mutual enrichment between Luther and Chauvet on the connection between sacraments and ethics, contributes in some small way to ecumenical conversations in sacramental theology and its connection to the ethical lives of Christians and the church.

Bibliography

Althaus, Paul, and Robert C Schultz. *Ethics of Martin Luther*. Minneapolis, MN: Fortress, 2007.

Ambrose, Glenn P. *The Theology of Louis-Marie Chauvet: Overcoming Onto-Theology with the Sacramental Tradition*. Surrey, England: Ashgate, 2012.

Aquinas, Thomas. *Summa Theologiae*.

Arendt, Hannah. *On Violence*. San Diego, CA: Harcourt Brace & Company, 1970.

Barth, Karl. *Church Dogmatics*. Vol. 1.1. Translated by G. W. Bromiley. Edited by G. W. Bromiley and T. F. Torrance. Peabody, MA: Hendrickson, 2010.

Baylor, Michael G. *The German Reformation and the Peasants' War*. New York: Bedford/St. Martin's, 2012.

Bethge, Eberhard. *Dietrich Bonhoeffer: A Biography*. Minneapolis, MN: Fortress, 2000.

Bevans, Stephen B. *Models of Contextual Theology*. Maryknoll, NY: Orbis, 1992.

Bonhoeffer, Dietrich. *Discipleship*. Minneapolis, Fortress, 2001.

———. *Ethics*. Minneapolis, MN: Fortress, 2009.

Bordeyne, Philippe. "The Ethical Horizon of Liturgy." In *Sacraments: Revelation of the Humanity of God*, edited by Philippe Bordeyne and Bruce T. Morrill, 119–36. Collegeville, MN: Liturgical Press, 2008.

Braaten, Carl E. *Principles of Lutheran Theology*. Minneapolis, MN: Fortress, 2007.

Brunk, Timothy M. *Liturgy and Life: The Unity of Sacraments and Ethics in the Theology of Louis-Marie Chauvet*. New York: Peter Lang, 2007.

Burgess, Joseph A., and Marc Kolden. "Introduction: Gerhard O. Forde and the Doctrine of Justification." In *By Faith Alone: Essays on Justification in Honor of Gerhard O. Forde*, edited by Joseph A. Burgess and Marc Kolden, 3–9. Grand Rapids, MI: Wm. B. Eerdmans, 2004.

Caputo, John D., and Michael J. Scanlon, eds. *God, the Gift, and Postmodernism*. Bloomington: Indiana University, 1999.

Chauvet, Louis-Marie. "Approche anthropologique de lEucharistie." In *Eucharistia: Encyclopédie de lEucharistie*, edited by Maurice Brouard, 21–32. Paris: Cerf, 2002.

———. *Du symbolique au symbole*. Paris: Cerf, 1979.

———. "L'avenir du Sacrementel." *Recherche de science religieuse* 75 (1987): 241–66.

———. "L'aveu dans le sacrement de la reconciliation: De l'absolution collective á la confession privée." In *L'aveu et la pardon: Expérience et réflexion chrétiennes*, edited by Louis-Marie Chauvet, M. Balleydier, and F. Deniau, 11–53. Paris: Chalet, 1979.

———. "La dimension sacrificielle de lEucharistie." *La Maison-Dieu* 123 (1975): 47–78.

———. "Le rite et l'éthique: Une tension féconde." In Louis-Marie Chauvet, et al. *Le rite, source et resources*, 137–55. Brussels: Facultés Universitaires Saint-Louis, 1995.

———. *Les Sacrements: Parole de Dieu au Risque du Corps*. Ivry-sur-Seine, France: Les Editions Ouvrieres, 1993.

———. "Le sacrifice comme échange symbolique." In *Le sacrifice dans les religions*, edited by Marcel Neusch, 277–304. Paris: Beauchesne Éditeurs, 1994.

———. "Parole et sacrement." *Recherche de science religieuse* 91 (2003): 203–22.

———. *Symbol and Sacrament*. Collegeville, MN: Liturgical Press, 1995.

———. *Symbole Et Sacrement*. Paris: Les Éditions du Cerf, 1987.

———. "The Broken Bread as Theological Figure of Eucharistic Presence." In *Sacramental Presence in a Postmodern Context*, edited by L. Boeve and L. Leijssen, 236–64. Leuven: Leuven University, 2001.

———. "The Liturgy in Its Symbolic Space." In *Liturgy and the Body*, edited by Louis-Marie Chauvet and Francois Kabasele Lumbala, 29–40. Maryknoll, NY: Orbis, 1995.

———. *The Sacraments: The Word of God at the Mercy of the Body*. Collegeville, MN: Liturgical Press, 1997.

Colombetti, Giovanna. *The Feeling Body: Affective Science Meets the Enactive Mind*. Cambridge: Massachusetts Institute of Technology, 2014.

Daly, Robert J. *Sacrifice Unveiled: The True Meaning of Christian Sacrifice*. New York: T&T Clark, 2009.

Day, Dorothy. "Adventures in Prayer." In *Dorothy Day: Selected Writings*, edited by Robert Ellsberg, 181–84. Maryknoll, NY: Orbis, 2002.

———. *Loaves and Fishes*. New York: Harper and Row, 1963.

———. *The Long Loneliness*. New York: HarperCollins, 1997.

De Certeau, Michel. *The Practice of Everyday Life*. Translated by Steven F. Rendall. Berkeley: University of California, 1988.

De Witte, Pieter. *Doctrine, Dynamic and Difference: To the Heart of the Lutheran–Roman Catholic Differentiated Consensus on Justification*. New York: Continuum, 2012.

Derrida, Jacques. *Given Time: I. Counterfeit Money*. Translated by Peggy Kamuf. Chicago: University of Chicago Press, 1992.

———. *The Gift of Death and Literature in Secret*. 2nd ed. Translated by David Wills. Chicago: University of Chicago Press, 2008.

———. *Writing and Difference*. Translated by Alan Bass. London: Routledge, 1978.

Dondaine, H. F. "A propos d'Avicenne et de S. Thomas: de la causalité dispositive á la causalité instrumentale." *Revue thomiste* 51 (1951): 441–53.

Dorrien, Gary. *Social Ethics in the Making: Interpreting an American Tradition*. Malden, MA: Wiley Blackwell, 2011.

Duffy, Stephen J. *The Dynamics of Grace: Perspectives in Theological Anthropology*. Collegeville, MN: Liturgical Press, 1993.

Ellsberg, Robert, ed. *Dorothy Day: Selected Writings*. Maryknoll, NY: Orbis, 2002.

Forde, Gerhard O. "The Critical Response of German Theological Professors to the Joint Declaration on Justification." *dialog* 38 (1999): 71–72.

———. *Justification by Faith: A Matter of Death and Life*. Philadelphia: Fortress, 1982.

———. "A Lutheran View of Sanctification." In *Christian Spirituality: Five Views of Sanctification*, edited by Donald Alexander, 13–32. Downers Grove, IL: IVP, 1988.

Forde, Gerhard, et. al. "A Call for Discussion of the 'Joint Declaration on the Doctrine of Justification.'" *dialog* 36 (1997): 224–29.

Forell, George Wolfgang. *Faith Active in Love: An Investigation of the Principles Underlying Luther's Social Ethics*. Minneapolis: Augsburg, 1954.

Forest, Jim. *All Is Grace: A Biography of Dorothy Day*. Maryknoll, NY: Orbis, 2011.

Fortuna, Joseph John. *Two Approaches to Language in Sacramental Efficacy Compared: Thomas Aquinas in the* Summa Theologiae *and Louis-Marie Chauvet*. PhD diss., The Catholic University of America, 1989.

Franklin, R. W., and Robert L. Spaeth. *Virgil Michel: American Catholic*. Collegeville, MN: Liturgical Press, 1988.

Gabrielli, Timothy R. "Chauvet in Space: Louis-Marie Chauvet's Sacramental Account of Christian Identity and the Challenges of a Global Consumer Culture." In *Religion, Economics, and Culture in Conflict and Conversation*, edited by Laurie Cassidy and Maureen H. O'Connell. Vol. 56 of the College Theology Society (2010): 134–56.

Hall, Jeremy. *The Full Stature of Christ: The Ecclesiology of Dom Virgil Michel*. Collegeville, MN: Liturgical Press, 1976.

Heidegger, Martin. *Introduction to Metaphysics*. Translated by Gregory Fried and Richard Polt. New Haven, CT: Yale University, 2000.

———. "Letter on Humanism." In *Basic Writings: Martin Heidegger*, edited by David Krell, 217–65. New York: HarperCollins, 1993.

———. *On the Way to Language*. New York: Harper & Row, 1982.

———. *Poetry, Language, Thought*. New York: HarperCollins, 2001.

———. "What Calls for Thinking?" In *Basic Writings: Martin Heidegger*, edited by David Krell, 369–91. New York: HarperCollins, 1993.

Hendrickson, Mark. *American Labor and Economic Citizenship: New Capitalism from World War I to the Great Depression*. New York: Cambridge University, 2013.

Hequet, Suzanne. *The 1541 Colloquy at Regensburg: In Pursuit of Church Unity*. Saarbrücken, Germany: VDM Verlag, 2009.

Herzfeld, Noreen. *Technology and Religion: Remaining Human in a Co-Created World*. West Conshohocken, PA: Templeton, 2009.

Hillenbrand, Reynold. "Address at the National Liturgical Week, Worcester, 1955." In *How Firm a Foundation: Voices of the Early Liturgical Movement*, edited by Kathleen Hughes, 134–35. Chicago: Liturgy Training Publications, 1990.

Joy, David, and Joseph Duggan, eds. *Decolonizing the Body of Christ: Theology and Theory after Empire?* New York: Palgrave Macmillan, 2012.

Kilmartin, Edward. *The Eucharist in the West*. Collegeville, MN: Liturgical Press, 2004.

Kretschmar, Georg. "Kreutz und Auferstehung in der Sicht von Athanasios und Luther." In *Der Auferstandene Christus und das Heil der Welt. Das Kirchberger Gespräch über die Bedeutung der Auferstehung für das Heil der Welt zwischen Vertretern der Evangelischen Kirche in Deutschland und Ruschischen Orthodoxen Kirche*, edited by Kirchliches Ausenamt der EKD, 40–82. Studienheft 7. Witten, 1972.

Lathrop, Gordon. *Holy Things: A Liturgical Theology*. Minneapolis, MN: Augsburg Fortress, 1993.

———. " 'Is That Your Liturgical Movement?' Liturgy and Sacraments in an Ecumenical Ecclesiology." In *Sacraments: Revelation of the Humanity of God*, edited by Philippe Bordeyne and Bruce T. Morrill, 101–14. Collegeville, MN: Liturgical Press, 2008.

Lazareth, William H. *Christians in Society: Luther, the Bible, and Social Ethics*. Minneapolis, MN: Fortress, 2001.

Leinsle, Ulrich G. *Introduction to Scholastic Theology*. Translated by Michael J. Miller. Washington, DC: The Catholic University of America, 2010.

Long, Michael G., ed. *Christian Peace and Nonviolence: A Documentary History*. Maryknoll, NY: Orbis, 2011.

López, Antonio. *Gift and the Unity of Being*. Eugene, OR: Wipf & Stock, 2013.

Luther, Martin. "Against the Robbing and Murdering Hordes of Peasants." Translated by Charles M. Jacobs. In *The Christian in Society III*, 49–56. Vol. 46 of *Luther's Works*. Edited by Robert C. Schultz and Helmut T. Lehmann. Philadelphia, PA: Fortress, 1967.

———. "An Open Letter on the Harsh Book Against the Peasants." Translated by Charles M. Jacobs. In *The Christian in Society III*, 63–86. Vol. 46 of *Luther's Works*. Edited by Robert C. Schultz and Helmut T. Lehmann. Philadelphia, PA: Fortress, 1967.

———. "A Sincere Admonition by Martin Luther to All Christians to Guard Against Insurrection and Rebellion, 1522." Translated by W. A. Lambert.

In *The Christian in Society II*, 51–74. Vol. 45 of *Luther's Works*. Edited by Walther I. Brandt and Helmut T. Lehmann. Philadelphia, PA: Fortress, 1962.

———. *Lectures on Galatians, 1535*. Vol. 26 of *Luther's Works*. Edited by Jaroslav Pelikan and Walter A. Hansen. Saint Louis, MO: Concordia, 1963.

———. *Lectures on Romans*. Vol. 25 of *Luther's Works*. Edited by Hilton C. Oswald. Saint Louis, MO: Concordia, 1972.

———. "Letter 91, to Philip Melanchthon, Wartburg, August 1, 1521." In *Letters I*. Vol. 48 of *Luther's Works*. Translated by Gottfried G. Krodel. Edited by Gottfried G. Krodel and Helmut T. Lehmann. Philadelphia, PA: Fortress, 1963.

———. *Luthers Werke auf CD-ROM*. Electronic reissue of the Weimar edition of D. Martin Luthers Werke. Cambridge, UK: Chadwyck-Healey, 2000.

———. *Sermons on the Gospel of John*. Vol. 24 of *Luther's Works*. Edited by Jaroslav Pelikan and Daniel E. Peollot. Saint Louis, MO: Concordia, 1961.

———. "Temporal Authority: To What Extent It Should be Obeyed, 1523." Translated by J. J. Schindel. In *The Christian in Society II*, 75–130. Vol. 45 of *Luther's Works*. Edited by Walther I. Brandt and Helmut T. Lehmann. Philadelphia, PA: Fortress, 1962.

———. "The Babylonian Captivity of the Church." In *Word and Sacrament II*, 3–126. Vol. 36 of *Luther's Works*. Edited by Abdel Ross Wentz and Helmut T. Lehmann. Philadelphia, PA: Fortress, 1959.

———. "The Freedom of a Christian." In *Career of the Reformer I*, 327–78. Vol. 31 of *Luther's Works*. Edited by Harold J. Grimm and Helmut T. Lehmann. Philadelphia, PA: Muhlenberg, 1957.

———. *The Large Catechism*. Translated by Robert H. Fischer. Philadelphia: Fortress, 1959.

———. "The Sacrament of the Body and Blood of Christ—Against the Fanatics." In *Word and Sacrament II*, 329–62. Vol. 36 of *Luther's Works*. Edited by Abdel Ross Wentz and Helmut T. Lehmann. Philadelphia, PA: Fortress, 1959.

———. *The Small Catechism*. In *The Book of Concord*, edited by Timothy J. Wengert and Robert Kolb, translated by Charles Arand, et al. Minneapolis, Fortress, 2000.

———. *The Smalclad Articles* (1537). In *The Book of Concord*, edited by Timothy J. Wengert and Robert Kolb, translated by Charles Arand, et al., 295–328 Minneapolis, Fortress, 2000.

Mann, Gary A. *Simul Iustus et Peccator: Luther's Paradigm of the Christian Life and Systematic Principle*. PhD diss., Drew University, 1988.

Mannermaa, Tuomo. *Christ Present in Faith: Luther's View of Justification*. Minneapolis: Fortress, 2005.

———. "Justification and Theosis in Lutheran-Orthodox Perspective." In *Union with Christ: The New Finnish Interpretation of Luther*, edited by Carl E. Braaten and Robert W. Jensen, 42–69. Grand Rapids, MI: Wm. B. Eerdmans, 1998.

———. "Why Is Luther so Fascinating? Modern Finnish Luther Research." In *Union with Christ: The New Finnish Interpretation of Luther*, edited by Carl E. Braaten and Robert W. Jenson, 1–20. Grand Rapids, MI: Wm. B. Eerdmans, 1998.

Marion, Jean-Luc. *Being Given: Toward a Phenomenology of Givenness*. Translated by Jeffrey Kosky. Redwood City, CA: Stanford University, 2002.

———. *God without Being*. Translated by Thomas A. Carlson. Chicago: University of Chicago, 1991.

Marx, Paul B. *Virgil Michel and the Liturgical Movement*. Collegeville, MN: Liturgical Press, 1957.

Mauss, Marcel. *The Gift: The Form and Reason for Exchange in Archaic Societies*. Translated by W. D. Halls. New York: W. W. Norton, 1990.

McElvaine, Robert. *Down and Out in the Great Depression*. Chapel Hill: The University of North Carolina, 1983.

McPartlan, Paul. *The Eucharist Makes the Church*. Fairfax, VA: Eastern Christian Publications, 2006.

Michel, Virgil. "Defining Social Justice." *The Commonweal* 23 (1936): 425.

———. "The Liturgical Movement of the Future." *America* 54, no. 1 (1935): 6–7.

Milbank, John. *Being Reconciled*. London: Routledge, 2003.

Miller, Vincent J. "An Abyss and the Heart of Mediation: Louis-Marie Chauvet's Fundamental Theology of Sacramentality." *Horizons* 24, no. 2 (Fall 1997): 230–47.

Morrill, Bruce. *Anamnesis as Dangerous Memory: Political and Liturgical Theology in Dialogue*. Collegeville, MN: Liturgical Press, 2000.

———, ed. *Bodies of Worship: Explorations in Theory and Practice*. Collegeville, MN: Liturgical Press, 2000.

———. *Divine Worship and Human Healing: Liturgical Theology at the Margins of Life and Death*. Collegeville, MN: Liturgical Press, 2009.

———. *Encountering Christ in the Eucharist: The Paschal Mystery in People, Word, and Sacrament*. New York: Paulist Press, 2012.

Mudd, Joseph C. *Eucharist as Meaning: Critical Metaphysics and Contemporary Sacramental Theology*. Collegeville, MN: Liturgical Press, 2014.

Murphy, Nancy, and Christopher C. Knight, eds. *Human Identity at the Intersection of Science, Technology, and Religion*. Burlington, VT: Ashgate, 2010.

Nepstad, Sharon Erickson. *Nonviolent Revolutions: Civil Resistance in the Late 20th Century*. New York: Oxford University, 2011.

Nichols, Aidan. *A Grammar of Consent*. Notre Dame, IN: University of Notre Dame, 1991.

Niebuhr, H. Richard. *Christ and Culture*. New York: HarperCollins, 1951.

Paulson, Steven D. *Lutheran Theology*. New York: Continuum, 2011.

Pecklers, Keith F. *The Unread Vision: The Liturgical Movement in the United States of America 1926–1955*. Collegeville, MN: Liturgical Press, 1998.

Piehl, Mel. *Breaking Bread: The Catholic Worker and the Origin of Catholic Radicalism in America*. Philadelphia: Temple University, 1982.

Polt, Richard. *Heidegger: An Introduction*. Ithaca, NY: Cornell, 1999.

Porter, Glenn. *The Rise of Big Business: 1860–1920*. 3rd ed. Hoboken, NJ: Wiley-Blackwell, 2005.

Powell, Jeffrey. *Heidegger and Language*. Bloomington: Indiana University, 2013.

Power, David. "The Word in Liturgy: Incarnating the Gospel in Cultures." In *Sacraments: Revelation of the Humanity of God*, edited by Philippe Bordeyne and Bruce T. Morrill, 47–62. Collegeville, MN: Liturgical Press, 2008.

Prenter, Regin. *Theologie und Gottesdienst: Gesammelte Aufsätze*. Arhus: Aros, 1977.

Quill, Timothy C. J. *The Impact of the Liturgical Movement on American Lutheranism*. Lanham, MD: The Scarecrow Press, 1997.

Reinhold, H. A. "A Social Leaven?" *Orate Fratres* 25 (1951): 515–18.

Ricoeur, Paul. *Memory, History, Forgetting*. Translated by Kathleen Blamey and David Pellauer. Chicago: University of Chicago, 2006.

Rowlands, Mark. *The New Science of the Mind: From Extended Mind to Embodied Phenomenology*. Cambridge: Massachusetts Institute of Technology, 2010.

Runyan, Jason D. *Human Agency and Neural Causes: Philosophy of Action and the Neuroscience of Voluntary Agency*. New York: Palgrave Macmillan, 2014.

Rynn, Xavier. *Vatican Council II*. Maryknoll, NY: Orbis, 1999.

Saliers, Don, and Emily Saliers. *A Song to Sing, A Life to Live: Reflections on Music as Spiritual Practice*. San Francisco, CA: Jossey-Bass, 2005.

Saliers, Don E. "Liturgy and Ethics: Some New Beginnings." In *Liturgy and the Moral Self: Humanity at Full Stretch Before God*, edited by E. Byron Anderson and Bruce T. Morrill. Collegeville, MN: Liturgical Press, 1998.

———. *The Soul in Paraphrase: Prayer and the Religious Affections*. Memphis, TN: Order of Saint Luke, 1991.

———. *Worship Come to Its Senses*. Nashville, TN: Abingdon, 1996.

Schmiesing, Kevin E. *Within the Market Strife: American Catholic Economic Thought from Rerum Novarum to Vatican II*. Lanham, MD: Lexington Books, 2004.

Schumacher, William W. *Who Do I Say That You Are? Anthropology and the Theology of Theosis in the Finnish School of Tuomo Mannermaa*. Eugene, OR: Wipf and Stock, 2010.

Scott, Tom, and Bob Scribner, eds. and trans. *The German Peasants' War: A History in Documents*. Amherst, NY: Humanity, 1991.

Seasoltz, Kevin. *God's Gift Giving*. New York: Continuum, 2007.

Senn, Frank C. *Christian Liturgy*. Minneapolis, MN: Fortress, 1997.

Severson, Eric R., ed. *Gift and Economy: Ethics, Hospitality and the Market*. Newcastle upon Tyne, UK: Cambridge Scholars, 2012.

Shusterman, Richard. *Thinking through the Body: Essays in Somaesthetics*. New York: Cambridge University, 2012.

Siemon-Netto, Uwe. *The Fabricated Luther: Refuting Nazi Connections and Other Modern Myths*. 2nd ed. Saint Louis, MO: Concordia, 2007.

Smith, Huston. *Beyond the Post-Modern Mind*. Wheaton, IL: The Theosophical Publishing House, 1982.

Sokolowski, Robert. *Phenomenology of the Human Person*. New York: Cambridge University, 2008.

Spivak, Gayatri Chakravorty. *An Aesthetic Education in the Era of Globalization*. Cambridge, MA: Harvard University, 2013.

Stephenson, George Malcolm. *The Conservative Character of Martin Luther*. Philadelphia, PA: The United Lutheran Publication House, 1921.

Tillard, J.-M.-R. *Church of Churches: The Ecclesiology of Communion*. Collegeville, MN: Liturgical Press, 1980.

———. *Flesh of the Church, Flesh of Christ: At the Source of the Ecclesiology of Communion*. Collegeville, MN: Liturgical Press, 2001.

The Lutheran World Federation. "Lutheran-Roman Catholic Dialogue." http://www.lutheranworld.org/content/lutheran-roman-catholic-dialogue (accessed February 22, 2014).

The Lutheran World Federation and The Catholic Church. *Joint Declaration on the Doctrine of Justifcation*. http://www.vatican.va/roman_curia/pontifical_councils/chrstuni/documents/rc_pc_chrstuni_doc_31101999_cath-luth-joint-declaration_en.html (accessed February 22, 2014).

The Lutheran World Federation and The Pontifical Council for Promoting Christian Unity. *From Conflict to Communion: Lutheran-Catholic Common Commemoration of the Reformation in 2017*. Leipzig, Germany: Evangelische Verlagsanstalt, 2013.

Townshend, Todd. *The Sacramentality of Preaching: Homiletical Uses of Louis-Marie Chauvet's Theology of Sacramentality*. New York: Peter Lang, 2009.

Tuzik, Robert. *Reynold Hillenbrand: The Reform of the Catholic Liturgy and the Call to Social Action*. Chicago: Liturgy Training Publications, 2010.

Upton, Julia A. *Worship in Spirit and Truth: The Life and Legacy of H. A. Reinhold*. Collegeville, MN: Liturgical Press, 2009.

Vatican Council II. *Apostolicam Actuositatem* (Decree on the Apostolate of Lay People). In *Vatican Council II: The Conciliar and Postconciliar Documents*, edited by Austin Flannery. Northport, NY: Costello, 2014.

———. *Sacrosanctum Concilium* (The Constitution on the Sacred Liturgy). In *Vatican Council II: The Conciliar and Postconciliar Documents*, edited by Austin Flannery. Northport, NY: Costello, 2014.

———. *Unitatis Redintegratio* (Decree on Ecumenism). In *Vatican Council II: The Conciliar and Postconciliar Documents*, edited by Austin Flannery. Northport, NY: Costello, 2014.

Walters, Brent. *From Human to Posthuman: Christian Theology and Technology in a Postmodern World*. Burlington, VT: Ashgate, 2006.

Weber, Wilhelm. *Simul Iustus et Peccator: Die Anthropologie der Rechtfertigungslehre Luthers*. Norderstedt, Germany: GRIN Verlag, 2013.

Wengert, Timothy, ed. *Centripetal Worship: The Evangelical Heart of Lutheran Worship*. Minneapolis: Augsburg Fortress, 2007.

White, Graham. *Luther as Nominalist: A Study of the Logical Methods Used in Martin Luther's Disputations in the Light of Their Medieval Background*. Helsinki, Finland: Luther-Agricola-Society, 1994.

White, James F. *The Sacraments in Protestant Practice and Faith*. Nashville, TN: Abingdon, 1999.

Wright, William J. *Martin Luther's Understanding of God's Two Kingdoms: A Response to the Challenge of Skepticism*. Grand Rapids, MI: Baker Academic, 2010.

Zizioulas, John D. *Being as Communion*. Crestwood, NY: St. Vladimir's Seminary, 1985.

————. *Communion and Otherness*. London: T&T Clark, 2006.

Zunes, Stephen, and Sarah Beth Asher, eds. *Nonviolent Social Movements: A Geographical Perspective*. Malden, MA: Blackwell, 1999.

Index